$12.00

Agriculture in Nicaragua

Promoting Competitiveness and
Stimulating Broad-Based Growth

THE WORLD BANK
Washington, D.C.

World Bank Country Studies are among the many reports originally prepared for internal use as part of the continuing analysis by the Bank of the economic and related conditions of its developing member countries and to facilitate its dialogues with the governments. Some of the reports are published in this series with the least possible delay for the use of governments, and the academic, business, financial, and development communities. The typescript of this paper therefore has not been prepared in accordance with the procedures appropriate to journal printed texts, and the World Bank accepts no responsibility for errors. Some sources cited in this paper may be informal documents that are not readily available.

The findings, interpretations, and conclusions expressed in this paper are entirely those of the author(s) and do not necessarily reflect the views of the Board of Executive Directors of the World Bank or the governments they represent. The World Bank cannot guarantee the accuracy of the data included in this work. The boundaries, colors, denominations, and other information shown on any map in this work do not imply on the part of the World Bank any judgment of the legal status of any territory or the endorsement or acceptance of such boundaries.

ISBN: 0-8213-5443-4
eISBN: 0-8213-5444-2
ISSN: 0253-2123

Cover Photograph by Carlos Arce.

Library of Congress Cataloging-in-Publication Data

Agriculture in Nicaragua: promoting competitiveness and stimulating broad-based growth.
    p. cm. -- (A World Bank country study)
    Includes bibliographical references.
    ISBN 0-8213-5443-4
    1. Agriculture--Economic aspects--Nicaragua. I. World Bank. II. Series.

HD1818.A37 2003
338.1'097285--dc21

2003042260

CONTENTS

LIST OF TABLES

FIGURES

BOXES

ABSTRACT

Agriculture in Nicaragua: Promoting Competitiveness and Stimulating Broad-Based Growth is part of the World Bank Country Study series. These reports are published with the approval of the subject government to communicate the results of the Bank's work on the economic and related conditions of the member countries to governments and to the development community.

Broad-based growth is one of the four pillars of the Nicaraguan Government's Poverty Reduction Strategy. Living standards of the rural poor will continue to depend largely upon agriculture. This study takes stock of major developments in Nicaragua's agricultural sector and argues that broad-based growth can be promoted by strengthening agricultural competitiveness. Export growth is the key, requiring immediate action within a coherent strategy. The case of coffee illustrates the proposed strategy. This report also identifies productivity constraints in rural factor markets, suggesting medium-and-long-term solutions. It concludes with a review of the issue of risk management and with descriptions of some promising pilot projects.

World Bank Country Studies are available individually or by subscription, both in print and on-line.

PREFACE

This is an advisory report addressed to policy makers in the Government of Nicaragua on how to turn the country's agricultural sector into an engine of broad-based economic growth. It is hoped the report may serve as a basis for policy dialogue between the Government, the private sector and the World Bank. This work has been financed by the World Bank with contributions from the Dutch, Swiss and Italian Governments.

Content and focus: This work summarizes extensive analyses prepared for the Government of Nicaragua by the World Bank and valuable work from PROVIA-IICA-USAID[1] (from now on referred to as PROVIA) with significant inputs from Government counterparts and other agencies.[2] It takes stock of major recent developments and it argues that much can be done through strengthening agricultural competitiveness to promote broad-based growth in Nicaragua, one of the four pillars of the Government's Poverty Reduction Strategy (PRSP). In the short to medium term, living standards of the rural poor will continue to depend largely on agriculture. Thus, broad-based growth in the agricultural sector is a necessary condition to build an exit path for the rural poor in Nicaragua.

Organization: An Introduction reviews the recent performance of the agricultural sector and describes key issues affecting its future. The issues can be divided into three groups, which are treated separately in each of the chapters that follow. Chapter 2 focuses on the competitiveness of Nicaraguan agricultural products. It argues that export growth is key to the sector's future and will require immediate action within a coherent strategy. Such a strategy is outlined in a "Roadmap" of short-term priorities for Government consideration. The case of coffee, Nicaragua's most important agricultural export commodity, is then used to illustrate the practical application of the proposed roadmap. Chapter 3 identifies problems constraining the productivity of rural factor markets-finance, land, labor and technology-and suggests solutions as part of an ongoing, medium- to long-term effort. Chapter 4 develops the concept of risk management in the sector and describes some current, promising pilot projects.

---

1. PROVIA (Programa de Fortalecimiento de las Capacidades del Sector Privado para la Formulación de Políticas) is a program financed by the United States Agency for International Development (USAID) through the Inter-American Institute for Cooperation on Agriculture (IICA).

2. The work draws from the World Bank Agricultural Sector Policy Note presented to the new administration and discussed in Managua in January, 2002. It also benefited from the outcome of a workshop carried out in February, 2002, in Managua with participation from Government counterparts, PROVIA and partner development agencies.

Acknowledgments

This study has been prepared by a World Bank team composed of Norman Piccioni (Senior Agricultural Economist and Task team Leader), Florencia Castro-Leal (Senior Economist, LCSPP), Carlos Arce and Alberto Valdés (Consultants). Inputs and background papers were provided by Panayotis Varangis (RDVCG), Piotr Mazurkiewicz (EXTCD), Paul Siegel, Andrea Serpagli, Lisa Taber, Manuelita Ureta, Jacob Yaron (Consultants), and Horacio Rose, Diana Saavedra, Alejandro Aráuz and Juan Rodríguez (PROVIA). Felipe Jaramillo, Martin Raine and Ulrich Lachler provided Management comments. Alain de Janvry and Shanta Devarajan provided comments to the Concept Paper as Peer Reviewers. Peter Brandriss and Andrea Semaan reviewed the final document.

The Governments of Switzerland, Italy and The Netherlands provided funds for the preparation of the background studies through TULUMSA, AGROTEC and the Free University of Amsterdam respectively. USAID through IICA financed the work of PROVIA.

Vice-President	David De Ferranti
Country Director	Jane Armitage
ESSD Director	John Redwood
Lead Economist	Carlos Felipe Jaramillo
Task Manager	Norman Bentley Piccioni

ABBREVIATIONS AND ACRONYMS

APL	Adaptable Program Lending
ATLMP	Agricultural Technology and Land Management Project
BAGSA	Commodity Exchange Market of Nicaragua
CEI	Center for Exports and Investments
CAFTA	Central America Free Trade Area
CGIAR	Consultative Group on International Agricultural Research
CIAT	Research Center on Tropical Agriculture
CIF	Cost, Insurance, Freight
CIMMYT	International Center for Improvements in wheat and maize
CSR	Corporate Social Responsibility
DAC	Communal Action Development
ENSO	Southern Oscillation
EPR	Effective Protection Rate
EPN	National Ports Enterprise
ESW	Economic Sector Work
FAITAN	Agricultural Research Competitive Fund
FAO	Food and Agriculture Organization
FAT	Agricultural Extension Competitive Fund
FCR	Rural Credit Fund
FISE	Emergency Social Funds
FNI	Nicaraguan Investment Fund
FSC	Forestry Stewardship Council
FOB	Free on Board
FONDEM	Fund for Municipal Development
FONDEN	Fund for National Disasters
FTAA	Free Trade Area of the Americas
FUNICA	Nicaraguan Foundation for Agricultural Technology
FTA	Free Trade Agreement
GAP	Good Agricultural Practices
GMP	Good Management Practices
GDP	Gross Domestic Product
GON	Government of Nicaragua
HACCP	Hazardous Analyses of Critical Control Points
HIPC	Highly Indebted Poor Country
IDR	Rural Development Institute
IICA	Inter-American Institute for Cooperation on Agriculture
INAFOR	National Forestry Institute
INATEC	National Institute of Technology
INIFOM	Nicaraguan Institute for Municipal Development
INTA	Nicaraguan Institute for Agricultural Technology
LSMS	Living Standard Measurement Survey
MAGFOR	Ministry of Agriculture, Livestock and Forestry
MIFIC	Ministry of Development, Industry and Commerce
MIS	Market Information System
MFN	Most Favoured Nation
Mz.	Manzanas

NAFTA	North America Free Trade Agreement
NGO	Non Governmental Organization
NPR	Nominal Protection Rate
OECD	Organization for Economic Co-operation and Development
OLADA	Latin America Organization for Energy
PA	Poverty Assessment
PROVIA	Program for Private Sector Strengthening and Policy Development
PRSP	Government's Poverty Reduction Strategy Paper
RFI	Rural Financial Intermediary
QMS	Quality Measurement System
QR	Quantitative Restrictions
QQ	Quintal
RAAN	Northern Autonomous Region of Nicaragua
SFIPO	Sustainable Forestry Investment Promotion Office
SIDA	Swedish Bilateral Cooperation
SINTA	National Agricultural Technology System
SIPMA	The Information System on Agricultural Prices and Markets
TOT	Terms of Trade
UNDP	United Nations Development Program
UNA	Agrarian National University
UNAN	Autonomous National University of Nicaragua
USAID	United States Agency for International Development
WB	World Bank
WTO	World Trade Organization

CURRENCY EQUIVALENTS

Currency Unit = Córdobas (Nicaragua)
US$1.00 = C$14.19

FISCAL YEAR
January 1 to December 31

EXECUTIVE SUMMARY

Though Nicaragua remains one of the poorest countries in its region, the country has made significant progress at reducing poverty over the last decade. The decline in poverty was most pronounced in the rural areas, where most of the poor are concentrated.

Poverty reduction in Nicaragua seems to be highly responsive to economic growth and a recent analysis strongly suggests that agriculture and agricultural policies over the last decade were among the key forces driving both strong overall economic growth and poverty reduction. In fact, the agricultural sector's rapid broad-based growth in the 1990s possibly represented the single most important cause of the significant poverty reduction that occurred between 1993 and 2001.

However, the causes of this growth—high export commodity prices, the availability of unoccupied land and a return to normalcy after a decade of civil war—were temporary. None of these factors can be expected to deliver a sustained growth impulse indefinitely. This means that growth in the rural sector, where most of the poor are concentrated, is likely to be short-lived in the absence of new stimuli to sustain agricultural output growth.

The coming prospect of regional economic integration poses unprecedented opportunities for the Nicaraguan agricultural sector. At the same time, it constitutes a tremendous challenge that will demand more pragmatic, timely policies to spur agricultural growth in a new direction: switching from an agricultural sector focused on producing extensive, low-productivity, traditional commodities, with low diversification and penetration in foreign markets, to a sector oriented more toward higher value-added, diversified, non-traditional commodities.

Placing primary emphasis on the first pillar of the Government Poverty Reduction Strategy Paper (PRSP), this advisory report suggests a framework conducive to boost exports and on the transition toward non-traditional and value-added agriculture, as the potential engine for future agricultural growth.

Some positive results could be achieved quickly. The areas for action recommended herein can be grouped in three categories, each of which is covered by a chapter in this report:

- Competitiveness
- Factor markets
- Risk management

Without action in these areas, it would be a mistake to believe that Nicaragua's strong agricultural growth of the 1990s can continue. Many factors that drove that growth will no longer apply in coming years, as described in this report's Introduction.

The report argues that Nicaragua's best hope for sustained growth and poverty reduction probably lies with agricultural exports. Within the agricultural sector, the largest sector of the country's economy, only exports have the potential to gain from opportunities in the world market. International demand potentially can fuel major, sustained growth to a degree that demand from the domestic market, a small market characterized by widespread poverty, cannot. Therefore, of the three main areas covered, this report accords greatest emphasis to improving competitiveness and recommends giving that goal highest priority.

Competitiveness

The high tradability of agriculture in Nicaragua and the modest size of its domestic market makes international markets crucial for the agriculture sector's performance. In spite of the small share of farmland devoted to the production of exportables (25 percent of harvested area), the total trade of agricultural goods (including the value of both imports and exports) accounted for almost 85 percent of agricultural GDP in 1998. This is high relative to several countries in the region.

Perhaps most promising for the future is the export performance of non-traditional agricultural products. Agricultural exports currently account for roughly 50-70 percent of total exports; but while the total value of traditional agricultural exports has declined over the past decade, the total value of non-traditional agricultural exports has quadrupled, now representing nearly one-third of agricultural exports.

What supports the potential for exports and non-traditionals in Nicaraguan agriculture? First, in the 1990s, agro-exports were shown to contribute strongly to overall economic growth and poverty reduction in Nicaragua (World Bank, 2000 and 2002). Second, rural employment, a basic precondition for broad-based growth, has increased more rapidly in Nicaragua with agro-exports. Agricultural exports are also relatively more labor intensive than import-competing agriculture. Exportables are less constrained in growth potential vis-à-vis production for the small Nicaraguan domestic market. Nicaragua is now more integrated into the world economy, so there is less protection for the production of importables (for example, more incentives to expand exports).

The chapter on competitiveness identifies four battlefronts where action should be taken to improve the competitiveness of Nicaraguan agricultural products:

- Modernizing Agribusiness
- Promoting Agricultural Exports
- Improving the Effectiveness of Public Spending
- Strengthening Public-Private Partnerships

Modernizing Agribusiness

The full positive impact of openness to trade in agriculture in Nicaragua beginning from the early 1990s has not been achieved due to market inefficiencies, bottlenecks in agricultural services and substantial deficiencies in productive infrastructure. Such restrictions translate into huge limitations and substantial unnecessary costs for doing agribusiness in Nicaragua.

Processing, sanitary management and market information systems are all examples of agricultural services that need improvement in Nicaragua. Although many sources of agricultural market information are currently operated in Nicaragua, producers' organizations complain of lacking the kind of information they need. A reduction of high transaction costs in bringing agricultural products to the market will require a shortening of the marketing chain (a stricter chain integration).

Meanwhile, despite considerable public spending on infrastructure during the 90s, Nicaragua continues to show considerable deficiencies in productive infrastructure that hamper the competitiveness of Nicaraguan agricultural products in foreign markets. Overcoming infrastructure bottlenecks in Nicaragua will necessarily require private sector participation. The public sector will need to find new ways of attracting private sector interest to invest in infrastructure and manage maintenance funds, for example, using foreign aid to leverage private-sector investment.

To promote modernization of agribusiness, government should grant highest priority to strategically *enlarging and upgrading domestic transport and utilities infrastructure*. The current market imperfections and the considerable implicit and explicit transaction costs can be greatly reduced by targeted policies and investments to improve transport and utilities infrastructure.

To achieve this goal, government should first focus on upgrading domestic power networks by stimulating the private sector to increase its current share of energy generation. ENEL should revise its electrical tariffs for agricultural uses to make them more easy to understand for producers, and consider the possibility of making them more affordable through transitional subsidies.

Second, MIFIC and MINEX should work together in developing a strategy to attract sea-carrier companies based on incentives and improved port services. EPN should continue current efforts to improve seaports, including exploring the possibility of developing a seaport on the Atlantic coast. MAGFOR and MIFIC in coordination with EPN should run effective awareness campaigns to stimulate use of domestic port facilities and services among the domestic business community.

Third, investments should be made as to complete the road linking the Pan-American Highway to Puerto Cabezas, to repair the road linking Corinto Port to Chinandega, to complete the road linking Muhan to El Rama, and to advance the development and maintenance of the secondary road system, linking villages and farms to primary roads. Direct involvement of local authorities ("Alcaldías") in these plans will greatly assure the correct road maintenance and access to eligible funds (for example, IDR and INIFOM/ FONDEM, among others).

Other suggested priorities are identified in Chapter 2, in the section A Roadmap for Increased Competitiveness in Agriculture.

Promoting Agricultural Exports

An analysis of the competitiveness of Nicaragua's main crops provides important guidance for trade policy: Nicaragua has already achieved good levels of trade liberalization, but this trend toward openness will need to continue. The country's agricultural growth will require a shifting of incentives to support production of non-traditional crops for export.

Analysis of the cost structures of Nicaragua's main crops, comparing their border price with their domestic price, reveals that a lowering of general tariff levels will tend to have little negative impact on producers of most crops. However, given the social dimension of some crops and their direct effect on the rural poor and on food security, support will be needed in some cases to help small-scale producers to make the transition to more competitive production processes or even to different, more competitive crops. Such support can come in the form of agricultural technology, improvements in physical infrastructure and other productive assistance; it can also come in the form of social protection programs, or support to alternative economic activities, rural or urban. Training programs and other "exit" support programs should also be included for those who will not make it.

Does openness to trade pose a risk of increased polarization in agriculture? Is there a risk of substantial dynamic growth among a subset of commercially oriented farmers, and a lack of dynamism among those less prepared to take advantage of the economic liberalization arising from economic reforms? Market reforms, including trade liberalization, are likely to have a differentiated impact on different sub-sectors of the agricultural sector. Although it is tempting to press for higher border protection (in the form of tariffs on imports, for example) in order to help small-scale farmers, arguing that they may be unable to switch flexibly to different cropping patterns, higher protection is not the only income policy option. On the contrary, in the long run, it may prove to be a counter-productive route. Alternative routes to assist this sub-sector include targeted programs aimed at improvements in roads, further developments in the financial sector, agricultural research and technology transfers, and initiatives to promote non-farm employment opportunities in rural areas.

Government highest priority in promoting agricultural exports should be granted to strategically *create the right incentives*. First, government should promote a series of policy measures to create the right environment. These policy measures would have political implications, and should be negotiated openly with the private sector. They would include abstention from direct price controls in inputs and final products and the reduction/leveling of tariffs over time, to allow the government to engage in a process of lowering transaction costs (as is already being accomplished on other fronts, such as economic infrastructure, energy and financial services), and to allow producers to adjust their production patterns to new market signals.

Second, government will need to creatively invest in direct incentives to support producers to stimulate successful transition to higher value-added activities. Examples of these incentives are the competitive funds for research, technical assistance, market studies, business plans preparation, etc. Direct transfers to farmers is not an option for Nicaragua, and it should be considered only as a measure of last resort.

Improving the Effectiveness of Public Spending

Both government and foreign aid expenditures in rural areas have been substantial, but they have not been cost-effective. Their high variability from year-to-year has undermined implementation, and this problem has been compounded by a lack of coordination among various Government ministries and donors.

The erratic nature of public funding spent on agriculture has undermined proper planning and efficient implementation: over the 1990s, the amount of agriculture spending varied from plus 157 percent of the level at which it began the decade to minus 32 percent. Thus, programs were not well coordinated and provided conflicting signals and incentives to various economic agents. Overall, projects funded were donor-driven largely due to the lack of a coherent rural development strategy.

It could be helpful to review best practices in other countries that have had some success in employing foreign aid effectively, particularly with respect to maintaining policy coherence, coordinating spending from different sources, and creating a results-oriented, spending management system.

To improve effectiveness of public spending, government should grant highest priority to strategically *coordinate effectively the use of donor resources*. Relative to the size of its population, Nicaragua is one of the countries with higher donors' contributions for public spending for the rural sector in in the world. Yet, there is a wide recognition that lack of focus, variability over time and space, and ever-changing agendas strongly affected the effectiveness of these investments in the last decade.

Besides making a serious effort to coordinate financial aid within a clearly defined, broadly discussed agricultural competitiveness agenda, as a second step government should develop specific indicators to measure the effectiveness of an export-promotion and broad-based growth strategy in agriculture. This can help guide all active agents in the sector, establishing investment priorities, particularly for donors who finance most of the capital budget.

Finally, strengthening the delivery mechanism of the Rural Development Institute (IDR, the key institution in charge of providing specialized, transitional support in the form of productive investments for small farmers) is possibly the single, most important policy measure that the government can take in the short term. IDR should support a portfolio of programs carefully targeted to help small producers raise their productivity and management capacity. Criteria should be aimed at securing higher returns to public investments and encouraging profitability of sub-projects. Managing few sectoral programs with narrow, well-targeted productive objectives might prove to be much more effective than the current practice. The government and the donor community have an excellent opportunity to support the IDR in this direction at a moment when major rural development programs are about to be refinanced with IDB, European Union, IFAD, FAO and bilateral donors. Recent discussions with IDR officials suggest the institution is already working in this direction, but the government needs to promote a more proactive role. Decisive action here will help gain the confidence of the donor community, encouraging donors to support such transition programs.

Strengthening Public-Private Partnerships

Any strategy to improve the sector competitiveness has a crucial pre-condition, that is to establish and strengthen successful partnerships among policy-makers and the domestic and foreign private sector. There are three reasons for this. First, successful partnerships between the public and the private sector create an enabling environment for the macro-sectoral economic policy. Private sector participation helps remove biases in economic policies against exports and agriculture, encourages the implementation of anti-monopoly measures to increase the competitive structure of the economy, and promotes active policy measures for cost-effective and efficient human resources development.

Second, successful partnerships between the public and the private sector share the costs and the risks of joint projects. Such co-operation can produce far greater benefits for both partners and for the country than a purely public or private sector investment. Public funds are used to mobilize and leverage private sector investments: development co-operation can thus become cheaper, more efficient and more sustainable in areas such as harvest, processing, packing, storage and shipment.

Third, successful partnerships between the public and the private sector can help to ensure the integration of the private sector's new role in social processes. Tri-lateral partnerships involving private companies, civil society and the state are a promising foundation for sustainable and structurally effective measures. The commonly recognized concept of Corporate Social Responsibility (CSR) can serve as a platform for such partnerships. When private enterprises, supported by other stakeholders, establish operations based on their social and environmental responsibility they tend to have a significant and long-term positive impact on local economies.

To develop Public-Private Partnerships, government should grant highest priority to *define key roles to be played by the public and private sectors in promoting competitiveness and removing constraints for exports.* Jointly, public and private sectors have key roles in promoting competitiveness and removing constraints for exports. The public sector has a crucial role in providing public goods, such as eliminating distortionary signals, providing infrastructure and facilitating information (such as market information). The private sector, domestic and foreign, needs to take the lead in identifying opportunities, facilitating the adoption of appropriate technologies, and making financial and marketing arrangements. Match-makers, such as individuals or firms with knowledge about local conditions and links with domestic and foreign investors, can also have a role in identifying opportunities and helping match domestic and foreign firms with producers. Important international lessons can be drawn from the on-going efforts in many countries to boost Corporate Social Responsibility (CSR).

Rural Factor Markets

While promoting the competitiveness of Nicaraguan agriculture should be at the heart of immediate policy measures to be undertaken by the current administration, these immediate measures will also have to be complemented by sustained, ongoing efforts, initiated over the past decade and still in progress, to improve factor market efficiency.

Four rural factor markets are examined here: finance, technology, land and labor. These markets function poorly, and in turn increase the costs of doing business and lower profitability. The social consequences are substantial: scant human capital (labor) plus minimal physical capital (partly due to lack of financing), low technology and unproductive land use translates into very low labor productivity; and thus wages are notoriously low.

Financial services are not accessible to or affordable for the majority of rural Nicaraguans, despite important reforms undertaken in recent years. Key contributing factors are the absence of a legal and regulatory framework and financial systems infrastructure to enable competition and cost-effective credit risk management among formal financial intermediaries, and the influx of large donor and government transfers that distort financial markets and have unintended distributional effects.

Technological packages in agriculture at the farm level are inaccessible or sub-utilized by most farmers (even if they have access to them). Lack of a coherent research agenda and institutional problems within and between the public and private sectors hamper effective delivery of extension and services. High illiteracy among farmers in part constrains demand for technology.

In land markets, despite the significant resources already spent towards securing land access and tenure of the poor, only one-third of claims have been resolved. Land tenure security is of broad importance due to its impacts on governance, productivity, welfare and overall economic efficiency. Land sales patterns are causing increased land concentration. Policy interventions, such as an effective land taxation, are needed to put economic pressure on large owners—not necessarily producers—to sell or to rent out their holdings.

Rural labor markets' major bottleneck comes from unskilled labor supply outstripping labor demand. To make labor more productive, government actions should focus on a combination of different policy instruments associated with education and technological change.

The following actions are recommended to improve rural factor markets:

a. *Facilitate rural finance by:* (i) establishing the legal, regulatory and incentive framework needed to facilitate competition among providers of like services and the safe expansion of savings, credit and payment services in rural areas; (ii) rationalizing government- and donor-financed support to the sector; (iii) providing regulatory and operational systems for the efficient use of credit information and movable property as loan collateral, thereby lowering the costs and risks associated with rural lending; and, (iv) investigating the barriers to increased capital mobilization through equity investments and innovative contractual arrangements in the rural sector.

b. *Boost access to technology by:* (i) repositioning INTA as a second-tier institution as well as direct provider of technological services of a strategic nature; (ii) giving political, technical and financial support to FUNICA; (iii) harnessing lessons learned from the on-going pilot experiences with competitive funding for agricultural research (FAITAN) and extension (FAT); (iv) developing a competitive market for agricultural training with participation of a broad array of service providers, including a new role for INATEC; and (v) increasing the flow of information, and effectively providing useful information services on agricultural technology to farmers and technicians.

c. *Improve land productivity by:* (i) giving priority to a systematic land-rights regularization program and making land rights registration accessible and affordable to the poor, (ii) establishing alternative conflict resolution mechanisms to resolve disputes over land, (iii) formulating the legal framework needed to identify and secure land tenure and use rights for indigenous peoples and ethnic minorities, (iv) addressing cooperative-sector issues speedily by facilitating the individualization of property rights, overcoming legal obstacles and confirming such rights on the ground, (v) completing institutional reforms in the land and property sector, and promoting sound land administration systems and procedures, and (vi) involving municipalities in providing land administration services.

d. *Raise labor market's human capital by:* (i) encouraging school attendance through feeding children at school, offering school uniforms, sparing families the costs of tuition and materials, (ii) bringing focus and coordination to the myriad nationally and internationally funded technical training programs, in part perhaps by linking such programs to the current work aimed at developing clusters of competitiveness, and (iii) encouraging employers to offer on-the-job training by lowering the minimum wage allowable to be paid to trainees, thus allowing the burden of training costs to be shared by employer and trainee.

Risk Management

Nicaragua's agricultural sector faces significant risks arising from highly frequent covariate shocks, such as natural disasters and economic shocks. Besides current efforts to prepare for natural disasters, at the national level by Defensa Civil and at the municipal level by Desarrollo de Acción Comunitaria, partnerships should be strengthened with the private sector and civil society to prepare for natural disasters. Recent economic shocks, such as the coffee crisis, and natural disasters like Hurricane Mitch and the regional drought, have highlighted the need to explore complementary market-based instruments to mitigate impact and mobilize additional resources and actors.

Improving Nicaragua's risk management capacity will involve, among other steps: enabling a favorable framework for private-sector provision of risk management tools (microfinance, insurance); promoting aggregation for distribution of crop insurance; validating pilot projects on weather-based and price insurance; and, exploring the purchase of catastrophic rainfall coverage by the government to assist specific extremely poor and vulnerable groups (provided public insurance criteria are transparent and do not crowd out private insurance, both approaches are complementary).

For the households most vulnerable to the agriculture sector's ongoing shocks and crises, short-term emergency relief efforts might wield even greater impact if they can be used simultaneously to channel risk reduction measures to those same beneficiary households, thus carrying longer-term benefits. The Emergency Social Funds (FISE) Project and community-based social funds could be one option for use.

The following actions are recommended to improve agricultural risk management:

a. *Encourage and enable rural financial institutions to offer innovative insurance products alongside credit services.* Insurance could be better integrated into a new, comprehensive rural finance strategy. There is also a need to focus attention on the risk management needs of rural financial institutions themselves. Promising, ongoing pilot studies on the provision of both weather-based insurance and commodity-price insurance through rural finance institutions are described this report's chapter on risk management.

b. *Improve forecasting, early warning and monitoring systems for agricultural risks, risk management practices, and outcomes.* Improved information on weather patterns, soil moisture, agro-ecological conditions etc. are needed to better forecast events that might negatively impact households. More information is needed on households' risk management strategies and capacities. Such information should help in efforts to reduce risks and reduce the impacts of such events. The Agricultural Technology Project can be mobilized for this purpose. Also, initiatives should be coordinated with other ministries (for example, MARENA, IDA) and organizations (for example, INITER).

c. *Improve knowledge about risks and risk management strategies for given groups of households, communities and localities.* The Natural Disaster Vulnerability Project and Rural Municipalities Project are good examples of such knowledge gathering.

d. *Recognize the potential for agricultural technology to serve risk management needs, integrating risk management into existing technology transfer programs.* Drought resistant technologies and improved water management practices for cash crops and food staples, along with improved storage and post-harvest technologies are examples. It is also critical to have a coordinated plan to improve rural education, research and training with respect to risk management options.

e. *Further improve the design and delivery of safety net systems, including improved targeting and monitoring systems.* Other considerations include the use of agricultural insurance such as weather based insurance and commodity price insurance as a means to fund safety net programs and to deliver assistance to the most vulnerable rural households.

f. *Consider the importance of risk and risk management when addressing other areas covered in this paper, such as:* stability in macroeconomic and policy regime, secure land tenure and use, flexible labor markets and labor mobility, improved marketing, transport and communications infrastructure.

SECTOR REVIEW AND KEY ISSUES

Poverty Reduction and Broad-Based Growth in Agriculture: The Challenge Ahead

Though Nicaragua remains one of the poorest countries in its region, with a per capita gross national product of only US$430, the country has made significant progress at reducing poverty over the last decade. The Living Standards Measurement Surveys (LSMSs) carried out for Nicaragua in 1993, 1998 and 2001 show a continuous decline in the proportion of the total population living under the poverty line. Nationally, poverty decreased steadily from 50.3 percent in 1993 to 45.8 percent in 2001. The decline in the share of the population living in extreme poverty is even more pronounced, having fallen from 19.4 percent in 1993 to 15.1 percent in 2001. The decline in poverty was most prominent in the rural areas, where most of the poor are concentrated, and especially in the Pacific and Central regions. In rural areas, poverty decreased from 76 to 68 percent from 1993 to 2001 (World Bank 2002).

If Nicaragua's poverty levels continue to decline at the same pace as during 1993–2001, the Millennium Development Goal (MDG) of cutting extreme poverty in half could be reached well before the target date of 2015.

Poverty reduction in Nicaragua seems to be highly responsive to economic growth: the upcoming Poverty Assessment update calculates elasticities of poverty to growth at 1.5 for overall poverty and almost 2 for extreme poverty for the entire period 1993 to 2001 (that is, every 1 percent increase in growth led to 1.5 and 2 percent decreases in poverty and extreme poverty, respectively) (World Bank 2002). The same analysis also suggests strongly that agriculture and agricultural policies over the last decade were among the key forces driving both strong overall economic growth and poverty reduction.

One key reason that growth in agriculture can be so effective at reducing poverty is the fact that the vast majority of Nicaraguan agricultural producers are small-scale producers, many of them currently poor. In fact, the agricultural sector's rapid broad-based growth in the 1990s possibly represented the single most important cause of the significant poverty reduction that occurred between 1993 and 2001 (World Bank 2002).

TABLE 1: POVERTY AND EXTREME POVERTY BY REGION, 1993, 1998, 2001								
	Incidence of Extreme Poverty (percentage)						Incidence of Poverty (percentage)	
Region 1993	1998	2001	1993	1998	2001			
National	19.4		17.3		15.1	50.3	47.9	45.8
Urban	7.3		7.6		6.2	31.9	30.5	30.1
Rural	36.3		28.9		27.4	76.1	68.5	67.8
Managua	5.1		3.1		2.5	29.9	18.5	20.2
Pacific								
Urban	6.4		9.8		5.9	28.1	39.6	37.2
Rural	31.6		24.1		16.3	70.7	67.1	56.8
Central								
Urban	15.3		12.2		11.1	49.2	39.4	37.6
Rural	47.6		32.7		38.4	84.7	74.0	75.1
Atlantic								
Urban	7.9		17.0		13.1	35.5	44.4	43.0
Rural	30.3		41.4		26.9	83.6	79.3	76.7

Source: World Bank 2001.

However, the causes of this growth—high export commodity prices, the availability of unoccupied land and a return to normalcy after a decade of civil war—were temporary. None of these factors can be expected to deliver a sustained growth impulse indefinitely, and indeed, Nicaragua's main export prices already have experienced a major deterioration since 2000.[3] The fact that overall poverty has continued to decline over 1998–2001 appears to be due mainly to the post-Mitch reconstruction boom, which also came to an end in 2001. This means that growth in the rural sector, where most of the poor are concentrated, is likely to be short-lived in the absence of new stimuli to sustain agricultural output growth.

The prospects for greater access by Nicaragua and other Central American countries to the consumer markets of their more developed NAFTA partners have improved with the recent integration initiatives associated with the Free Trade Area of the Americas (FTAA) and a possible Central America Free Trade Area (CAFTA). The coming prospect of regional economic integration poses unprecedented opportunities for the Nicaraguan agricultural sector. At the same time, it constitutes a tremendous challenge that will demand more pragmatic, timely policies to spur agricultural growth in a new direction: switching from an agricultural sector focused on producing extensive, low-productivity, traditional commodities, with low diversification and shallow penetration in foreign markets, to a sector oriented more toward higher value-added, diversified, non-traditional export commodities.

This report therefore places primary emphasis on the transition toward non-traditional and value-added agriculture and on ways to boost exports as the potential engine for future agricultural growth. This emphasis on exports is recommended because only the vast demand of external markets can fuel the sustained production growth needed for meaningful poverty reduction. Domestic demand does not have the same potential to fuel sustained growth, because Nicaragua's domestic market is small and characterized by widespread poverty. However, in world markets, traditional agricultural products are highly protected by the U.S., Europe and Japan. For this reason, a focus on non-traditional crops is recommended for Nicaragua.

---

3. Accordingly, poverty has increased again over 1998-2001 in the principal coffee growing areas (Central Rural region), which are the ones that suffered the greatest price shocks.

**BOX 1: NICARAGUA'S POVERTY REDUCTION STRATEGY:
GROWTH AS THE FIRST PILLAR OF THE PRSP**

*Since 1990, government policies have been guided by a vision of a stable market economy in which the private sector
becomes the main engine of both growth and poverty*

Pillar: Broad-Based Economic Growth and Structural Reform

This pillar focuses on the following actions:

- Improving incentives for rural development through the elimination of price and cost distortions faced
  by farmers.
- Securing property rights and improving the operation of rural factor markets to encourage private investment.
- Increasing investments in rural infrastructure.
- Implementing programs aimed at small and medium-sized producers, through a strategy of fostering
  competitiveness in several strategic clusters with high growth potential.
- Promoting improved production technologies to raise agricultural productivity growth.

While an effective means for overall poverty reduction, the growth path suggested in this
report is more likely to favor the population segment of non-extreme poor, rural inhabitants
(those whose income places them between above the extreme poverty line but below the moderate
poverty line), leaving pockets of the extreme poor behind. Thus, the recommendations of this
report must be carefully balanced with public spending programs to invest in human capital, social
protection and safety nets.

We begin by describing the sector's structure, recent performance and socioeconomic importance, including its central role in poverty reduction, and then identify key issues that will need to
be addressed in order to unleash sustainable growth.

The Sector's Structure and Recent Performance

The share of gross national product coming from agriculture is larger in Nicaragua than in any
other Central American country, and the sector's strong growth in the 1990s made its contribution to gross national product rise to 30 percent by 2000.

Most of the agricultural sector is devoted either to basic staple grains or to export crops, two
separate categories which differ in the amount of land they consume and in the amount of value
they contribute to agricultural GDP. Land use is dominated by the basic staple grains, mostly rain-
fed: about 80 percent of cultivated land is planted with corn, beans, rice, and sorghum. In contrast,
only about 20 percent of cultivated land is devoted to export crops: coffee, sesame, sugar, tobacco,
and peanuts. However, basic staple grains contribute only about 30 percent of agricultural GDP
(according to 2000 figures), while export crops contribute some 50 percent (BCN 2001).

TABLE 2: AGRICULTURAL GNP
(As a Percentage of Total GNP)

Country	1997	1998	1999	2000
Nicaragua	28.5	28.3	28.4	30.0
Costa Rica	18.0	17.9	n.a.	14.5
El Salvador	13.5	12.8	10.4	13.0
Guatemala	24.3	24.0	23.1	20.2
Honduras	29.3	27.8	24.1	20.2

Source: PROVIA 2002.

As for livestock and horticultural crops: livestock production continues to be of the extensive type and is mostly for domestic consumption (though some is exported, and there is potential for expansion of these exports); and horticultural crop is limited, much of it also for domestic consumption. The contribution of livestock, mainly cattle, poultry, and pigs, to agricultural GDP and employment ranged between 5 and 10 percent during the 1990s. Livestock is also used as an important mechanism for savings and risk management by rural households: over 20 percent own cattle, over 60 percent own poultry and over 30 percent own pigs.

Nicaragua's agricultural sector achieved a remarkably high rate of growth during the 1990s, but it is important to recognize that much of this growth was due not to productivity gains but to expansion of the total area under cultivation (Table 3).

Period	Annual average agricultural growth (%)	Annual average increase in harvested land (%)
1960–1970	6.49	2.91
1970–1980	1.90	0.94
1980–1990	-2.13	1.09
1990–2000	6.35	4.31

TABLE 3: ANNUAL AVERAGE RATES OF AGRICULTURAL GROWTH AND HARVESTED AREA

Source: PROVIA 2002.

The country registered 6.35 percent annual growth in agricultural activity during the early 1990s. By 2000, agricultural growth had reached an annual average of 7.6 percent, surpassing the agricultural growth rates of its Latin American neighbors. While coffee production played a critical role in raising the national agricultural average output, overall exports from the agricultural sector grew from 1990 to 2000 by only 20 percent, a disappointing achievement compared with agricultural export performance in many if not most countries in Latin America.

However, this overall exports performance conceals a significant difference between the performance of traditional exports and non-traditional exports. Traditionals' modest growth in the first part of the 1990s was more than offset by a decline in the second half of the decade. In contrast, non-traditional exports grew strongly throughout, quadrupling by the end of the decade.[4]

Agricultural exports account for roughly 50–70 percent of Nicaragua's total exports. Coffee exports alone (which in 2000 were some 62 percent of agricultural exports) account for 25–30 percent of total exports.

Coffee has been a major engine of growth for Nicaragua, contributing some 5.3 percent of GDP in the 1990s, and accounting for 32 percent of rural employment. About 30,000 households grow coffee and another 150,000–200,000 households receive some part of their income as full-time or part-time laborers in coffee production, processing and marketing. The combination of coffee production plus fishery output has averaged 40 percent of total exports in the last three years, despite the drop in coffee prices in recent years (PROVIA 2002). With international coffee prices at historic lows, the weaknesses of this sub-sector are contributing to a crisis; but coffee will continue to be critical to any broad-based agricultural growth strategy and thus deserves special attention.

Agricultural production in Nicaragua is characterized by low factor productivity, as evidenced, in part, by stagnant-declining real agricultural wages (1994–99).[5] The agricultural sector employs

---

4. Traditionals initially grew from US$239 million in 1990 to US$247 million in 1995, then fell to US$225 million by 2000. Non-traditionals grew strongly throughout, from US$19 million in 1990 to US$33 million by 1995 and US$85 million by 2000.

5. Low agricultural wages in Nicaragua are also a function of the high supply of unskilled labor in rural areas and the lack of non-agricultural employment opportunities.

TABLE 4: AVERAGE ANNUAL PRODUCTION OF BASIC GRAINS

Product	Unit	1994/95	1995/96	1996/97	1997/98	1998/99	1999/2000
Rice							
Area	Mz. × 1000	83	90	97	105	120	88
Production	QQ × 1000	2501	2171	3149	3580	3803	2989
Yield	QQ/Mz.	30.0	24.1	32.6	34.0	31.7	34.0
Red beans							
Area	Mz. × 1000	172	150	171	193	270	296
Production	QQ × 1000	1840	1500	1647	1574	3280	2959
Yield	QQ/Mz.	10.7	10.0	9.6	8.2	12.1	10.0
Maize							
Area	Mz. × 1000	280	320	399	333	361	365
Production	QQ × 1000	5320	6400	7103	5810	6610	6441
Yield	QQ/Mz.	19.0	20.0	17.8	17.4	18.3	17.6
Sorghum							
Area	Mz. × 1000	70	38	77	77	59	61
Production	QQ × 1000	2000	1063	2655	1913	1131	1692
Yield	QQ/Mz.	28.6	27.3	34.5	24.9	19.2	27.7

Mz. = *manzana*. 1.431 *manzanas* is equivalent to 1 ha. QQ = *quintales*. 1 Q is equivalent to 46.36 kg.
Source: BCN 2001.

more than 40 percent of workers in Nicaragua. Real agricultural wages are on average about half of non-agricultural wages, around 1000 *córdobas* (roughly US$80) per month.

Agricultural production uses little capital in terms of machinery and equipment. Nicaragua's rates of agricultural machinery use are low compared to other countries in the region. Data from 1979–81 show Nicaragua was using, on average, 6 tractors per thousand hectares; this number rose to 7 in

TABLE 5: PRODUCTION OF KEY AGRICULTURAL EXPORT PRODUCTS

Product	Unit	1994/95	1995/96	1996/97	1997/98	1998/99	1999/2000
Coffee							
Area	Mz. × 1000	105	120	121	127	128	143
Production	QQ (oro) × 1000	920	1201	1100	1430	1440	2083
Yield	QQ/Mz.	8.8	10.0	9.1	11.3	11.2	14.5
Sugar							
Area	Mz. × 1000	60	64	71	75	77	80
Production	TC × 1000 /1	2853	3518	4015	4126	3805	4056
Yield	TC/Mz.	47.8	55.0	56.2	55.3	49.7	50.8
Bananas							
Area	Mz. × 1000	2.4	2.5	2.5	2.5	2.8	2.5
Production	Boxes × 1000 /2	2230	3384	4634	4866	4603	3932
Yield	Boxes/Mz.	929	1353	1854	1946	1650	1605
Sesame							
Area	Mz. × 1000	39	53	37	17	11	12
Production	QQ × 1000	375	418	223	148	69	90
Yield	QQ/Mz.	9.6	7.9	6.0	8.6	6.2	7.8

1/ TC= short ton (907.18 Kg.)
2/ boxes of 42 pounds
Source: BCN 2001 and World Bank staff estimates.

TABLE 6: AGRICULTURAL SECTOR STRUCTURE AND TRENDS—SELECTED INDICATORS			
	1990	1995	2000
Gross domestic product, at constant prices (=1980)	100.0	100.0	100.0
Primary Sector GDP / GDP Total (=1980) \1	24.7	27.7	29.5
Agriculture & Livestock / GDP Total (=1980)	24.2	25.0	27.5
Agriculture/GDP Total (=1980)	15.9	17.4	19.3
Agriculture/Primary Sector GDP	64.2	65.4	65.3
Livestock/GDP Total (=1980)	8.31	8.4	8.22
Livestock/Primary Sector GDP (=1980)	33.5	34.5	27.8
Total Export/GDP market price	29.6	25.2	26.9
Primary Exports Total Merchandise Exports	79.2	71.3	64.0
Agricultural Exports/Total Merchandise Exports	72.3	53.1	42.9
Coffee & lobster exports/Primary Exports	30.5	57.3	68.4
Coffee Exports/Agricultural Exports	29.7	53.1	61.8
Agricultural Imports/Total imports	7.7	5.6	5.9
Industrial imports/Total imports	28.7	41.7	31.7
Transport sector imports \2 / Total imports	16.4	7.2	10.2
Oil and derivatives imports / Total imports	19.1	15.1	16.2
Agriculture & livestock employment / Total employment	38.7	39.5	42.5

\1 Primary sector includes agriculture, livestock, fishing and forestry.
\2 Transport sector imports include intermediate and capital goods imports, it excludes oil and derivatives.
Source: BCN 2001.

1994–1996. In comparison, neighboring Costa Rica was using 22 and 23 tractors, respectively, in those two time periods. Nicaraguan fertilizer consumption is also low when compared to other countries in the region. In 1979–81, Nicaragua was consuming 392 grams of fertilizer per hectare of arable land. This consumption decreased to 147 grams per hectare in 1995–97. Costa Rica, in contrast, consumed 2,650 grams in 1979–81, and this rose to 3,636 in 1995–97. These figures show the low intensity of agricultural production in Nicaragua, representing great potential for either diversifying into organic farming and/or moving into high input, high output agriculture.

The Sector's Socioeconomic Importance

Rural poverty is highly correlated with agricultural production: that is, many rural households receiving a high proportion of income from agricultural activities are poor. The existence of pervasive poverty throughout the economy limits the potential for domestic demand for agricultural products— especially for higher-value non-staple foods—to serve as a major source of demand-driven growth.

The distributions across Nicaragua's population of income, land, assets in general, education and access to markets are characterized by high inequality, despite years of struggle for more equity (Corral and Reardon 2001).[6,7] Assets, incomes and opportunities are also unequally

---

6. Some Gini coefficients measuring inequality of different types in Nicaragua are revealing: 0.60 for national income, 0.86 for land, 0.80 for cattle (a Gini of zero indicates perfect equality, and a Gini of 1.0 indicates perfect inequality, wherein one person owns everything) (Davis and Murgai 2001:13).

7. According to Corral, Reardon (2001), two thirds of farms are below 5 manzanas in size and occupy one twentieth of total farmland; while one tenth of farms are 50 manzanas and above, controlling three fourths of total farmland.

distributed in geographical terms, concentrated in the Pacific Macro-Region (Corral and Reardon 2001). As in much of Latin America, this high degree of inequality gives rise to a strongly dualistic agricultural sector. Large numbers of low-skilled, low-paid farm laborers, landless or with small landholdings, compete for employment in the agricultural sector. The high inequality in the agricultural sector makes it important to analyze—*ex-ante* and *ex-post*—the distributional impacts of policy reforms.

The agrarian structure of Nicaragua is highly dualistic. This vastly complicates the task of promoting broad-based growth because policies are likely to have highly differentiated impacts, with difficult trade-offs between the poor and non-poor. Davis and Murgai (2000) describe the distribution of land across five categories of rural population. The categories are defined in terms of the amount of land owned, given in terms of manzanas (mz.), and for each, the percentage of total rural households belonging in that category is shown: (i) the landless, 38 percent; (ii) minifundio (up to 2 mz.), 13 percent); (iii) small farmers (2–5 mz.), 21 percent; (iv) medium farmers (5–20 mz.), 15 percent; and (v) large farmers (above 20 mz.), 13 percent. The rural poor are virtually all those in the first two categories (landless and minifundio) and many of those in the third category (small farmers). These categories constitute 72 percent of rural households but account for only 16 percent of total land. They not only have limited land assets but also low levels of education. This combination of poor access to land and low human capital assets broadly characterizes the poor in rural Nicaragua. The medium and large farmers constitute 28 percent of rural households but own 84 percent of total land.

These socioeconomic dimensions of rural poverty in Nicaragua highlight the critical importance of the agricultural sector in any broad-based strategy to reduce poverty. Unless the dualistic structure of agricultural production in rural areas is tackled, the poor, the landless, the subsistence farmers and other small-scale farmers may benefit only slightly from overall growth in the sector. Thus, growth-oriented policies will need to be complemented by public spending targeted to investment in human capital among the poor and social protection programs. At the same time, the government's ongoing efforts to improve the functioning of rural factor markets, as discussed in this document's second chapter, will be needed if agricultural growth is to be pro-poor: land reform, and expansion of microfinance availability constitute factor-market improvements that have the potential to reduce the dualistic structure of Nicaraguan agricultural production.

Key Issues on Agricultural Exports

Why the focus on agricultural exports? Because only they can drive Nicaragua's future economic growth and poverty reduction. There are three reasons for this. First, the sheer size of the agricultural sector within Nicaragua's economy means that strong growth in agriculture is a necessary condition for any broad-based, overall economic growth. Second, given a domestic market that is small and characterized by widespread poverty, only the vast demand of external markets can fuel the sustained Nicaraguan production growth needed for poverty reduction. Third, export crops in Nicaragua have strong backward and forward linkages from farm inputs, harvesting, post-harvesting and marketing. In fact, it is the economic activity linked to agricultural exports that constitutes, in many areas of the country, the bulk of the non-agricultural sector. These important multiplier effects are a major source of rural employment.

However, the international competitiveness of Nicaraguan agricultural exports is constrained in numerous ways.

Marketing constraints. Nicaraguan agricultural products have faced adverse conditions on world markets over the last few years, but their poor market performance can also be attributed to a number of controllable factors. Low levels of organization and integration of the sector's vertical chains; lack of, inadequate, or difficult access to marketing resources; high transaction costs; partial impact of existing market information systems; limited use of sales procedures; limited implementation of quality and sanitary management systems and concepts; high prices for fuel and marketing costs; and difficulty to procure quality packaging materials produced domestically are the main constraints faced today by key economic players in agriculture (Serpagli 2002).

Poorly performing goods markets. Wide regional differences in the costs of inputs, and in the farm-gate prices received by different types of farmers (and by farmers in different regions) is evidence that market segmentation is pervasive. High commercial margins for staple grains, fruits and vegetables, reveal inefficiencies in marketing structure (Serpagli 2000). Indeed, evidence on the functioning of two major staples, corn and beans, shows that they are segmented and transaction costs are high (Davis and Murgai 2000). This situation may be attributed in part to the fact that the functioning of agricultural markets for corn and beans was subject to large swings in government intervention: state control to replace private intermediaries prevailed under the Sandinista government (1979–90), but was replaced with the dismantling of state controls under the Chamorro government (1990–96). Whatever the cause, the result is the same: transaction costs rise and opportunities for profitable production are reduced.

Insufficient infrastructure. Lack of access to basic services and infrastructure poses serious limitations to improved competitiveness. The difference in access to electricity services between urban and rural areas in Nicaragua is stark. In urban regions access to this utility ranges from 68 percent to 56 percent of the total population, as compared to 17 percent and 36 percent in the Atlantic and North of the country respectively. With more than half of the country's population without access to this service, processing plants (coffee, for example), modern communication technology (fax and internet, and access to the information market and technical information) and production equipment (pumping of water for irrigation purpose) are not an option (Serpagli 2002). The Atlantic and the Pacific parts of the countries also lack an adequate telecommunications infrastructure. The number of telephone lines for every thousand inhabitants in the Atlantic region is 20.3 per thousand - a sharp contrast when compared to the Central part of the country, which covers 73.7 telephone lines per thousand.

Anti-export incentives. High Nominal Protection Rates for a select group of importable commodities constrain any agro-export strategy by creating price signals that make production of importables more attractive than production of exportables.[8] Current Nominal Protection Rates of 38 percent for importables in the agricultural cycle 2001/2002 are maintained, mainly to protect domestic producers from recent drops in international commodity prices. Trade liberalization had in fact exposed the low productivity and high transaction costs of domestic markets, factors that are important contributors to the non-competitiveness of import substitutes. The high protection rates for importables stand in contrast with the negative protection rates showed for exportables.

Additionally, the Córdoba has recently experienced some degree of appreciation with respect to the dollar, due to a slowing down of the rate of crawling-peg depreciation. As a result, although domestic producers of both importables and exportables had been benefiting from higher domestic prices between 1994–1998, their products have undergone a slight decline in competitiveness thereafter. Still, the Córdoba's appreciation has not been great enough to become a fundamental constraint on the agricultural sector. While the (real) exchange rate (RER) is the most influential "price" affecting the agricultural economy, government policies can do little to control the RER but hopefully the combined impact of trade, fiscal and monetary policies will lead to a relatively "high" and relatively stable RER (Valdés 2001).

Ineffective public spending. Fiscal policy and public expenditures in rural areas have not reversed the anti-export incentives or raised competitiveness even though on balance agriculture has received

---

8. Nominal rate of protection (NRP) = 100 (Pi-Pw)/Pw, where Pi= domestic price and Pw= world price. Effective rate of protection (ERP)= 100 (VAi-Vaw)/Vaw, where Vai= value added with protection and Vaw= value added under free conditions. When the NPR is greater than zero, the domestic price is high relative to the world price and producers are being benefited while consumers are effectively being taxed. When NPR is less than zero, producers are effectively being taxed and consumers are being subsidized. ERP measures are useful to examine the resource pull between agriculture and other sectors.

TABLE 7: ESTIMATES OF AGRICULTURE PROTECTION IN NICARAGUA
(At Official Exchange Rate)

Crop Cycle	Nominal Protection Rate %	Effective Protection Rate %
Importables		
96/97	11	13
97/98	56	75
98/99	51	68
99/00	31	65
00/01	47	66
00/02	38	57
Exportables		
96/97	-3	-1
97/98	-4	-2
98/99	-1	-4
99/00	1	1
00/01	-1	-1
00/02	1	-1

Source: PROVIA (2002).

favorable treatment from fiscal policy and public expenditures. The explicit taxes paid by agriculture are low—less than 7 percent of total gross revenues—and the sector benefits from 10 percent of total tax exemptions. Moreover, substantial funds, mostly financed by grants from external sources, have been spent on agriculture and on developing rural areas. At the same time, current and capital expenditures have risen from 2.6 percent of Central Government spending in 1991 to 8.4 percent in 2001, rising from about US$11 million in 1991 to US$79 million in 2001, or from 0.7 percent to 2.3 percent of GDP (World Bank 2001a). Despite this public investment, there has not been a major boost to competitive agricultural production. Why? There are two major reasons. One is the incoherence of the overall incentive system for a country that has embraced trade openness and integration in the global market. Although the net outflow/inflow ratio indicates net inflow of resources into agriculture, it does not take into account implicit taxes through trade taxes and exchange rate overvaluation. Two, the way in which public expenditures are managed makes cost-effective use virtually impossible. The erratic nature of funding—the annual variation in funding varied from plus 157 percent to minus 32 percent—has undermined proper planning and efficient implementation. Thus although there have been a variety of programs, their effectiveness is highly questionable. The programs are not coordinated, provide conflicting signals and incentives to various economic agents, and lack systematic monitoring and evaluation data. Overall, projects have been donor-driven rather than target-group driven, largely due to the lack of a coherent rural development strategy.

Poorly performing factor markets. When rural factor markets work well, they may play a critical role in linking economic growth to rural poverty reduction. This would be particularly true in the dualistic structure of rural Nicaragua. However, in the four factor markets considered in this report—rural finance, agricultural technology, land and rural labor—effectiveness and productivity are low. In rural finance and in the land market, policy reforms and an improved regulatory environment are long overdue. In the rural labor market, educational levels and worker productivity, and hence wages, are all notoriously low. Insufficient investment in technology generation and adaptation constrains productivity.

High vulnerability to external shocks. Nicaragua's agricultural sector faces significant risks arising from highly frequent shocks, often coming simultaneously in more than one form, ranging from market-induced shocks to policy-based and natural shocks. The Nicaraguan economy's high exposure to risks leads to a high degree of vulnerability, from the national level down to the household level, due to a lack of risk-management capacity. Examples of risks and shocks are numerous and diverse. For instance, terms of trade plummeted from 102 to 73 in 1996–1999 (1995=100), when world prices for coffee (a Nicaraguan export) declined steeply while world prices for oil (a Nicaraguan import) rose sharply. Nicaragua's vulnerability to market risks through trade increased as its "degree of openness" increased from 7 percent to 11 percent over the 1993–1999 period. Vulnerability to risk is also high due to the high proportion of export earnings depending on so few commodities: coffee accounts for 30 percent of export earnings, and shrimp and lobster account for 20 percent (2000 figures). Moreover, Nicaragua's heavy indebtedness is a source of vulnerability: its debt of US$6.6 billion requires debt servicing equivalent to 44 percent of total exports of goods and non-factor services (2000). Finally, Nicaragua's vulnerability to natural disasters obvious and extreme, with recent disasters including Hurricane Joan in 1988, a tidal wave in 1992, volcanic eruptions in 1992 and 1994, El Niño in 1996–1998, Hurricane Mitch in 1998, droughts in 1996 and 2001 and floods in 2002.

2

PROMOTING COMPETITIVENESS

There is compelling evidence that openness to trade is associated with increased growth. Countries that chose openness in the last decade experienced higher rates of growth compared with relatively more closed economies. In fact, trade has driven much global growth for the past thirty years and has proven to be a powerful strategy for developing countries. For agriculture, the period has seen a tenfold increase in global exports.

Dynamism in international agricultural trade has come mainly from a growing market for non-traditional products. In traditional products, most developing countries face an environment of significant protectionism by developed countries. OECD subsidies pay about $350 billion a year on agricultural subsidies, or some $309 per acre. The recent farm bill approved by the US Congress is about $180 billion over ten years or about $49 per acre.[9] This new bill subsidizes products that are important to developing countries, not only raising subsidies but also introducing new ones and reintroducing others that had been eliminated in 1996. Subsidies are raised for large staple crops, such as soybeans, wheat and corn, and for cotton. New subsidies are for dairy farms, peanuts, chickpeas and lentils. Reintroduced subsidies are honey, wool and mohair.

In this global environment, small open economies such as Nicaragua's must proactively seek access to foreign markets of agricultural products by increasing their share of non-traditionals. This poses a set of new challenges and opportunities for both the private and public sectors. A new competitiveness agenda in Nicaragua, including cluster development, has recently received considerable private and public support. Its emphasis on private-sector modernization, public-sector reform and private-public partnerships has great potential. This clusters policy, with the right components, can become the key to promoting the increased level of competitiveness Nicaragua requires to access those markets.

---

9. The "Farm Security and Rural Investment Act of 2002" replaces the "FAIR Act of 1996" and sets out various agricultural programs under 10 titles, notably the commodity (farm subsidy) programs, conservation and trade.

What supports the potential for exports and non-traditionals in Nicaraguan agriculture? First, in the 1990s, agro-exports were shown to contribute strongly to overall economic growth and poverty reduction in Nicaragua (World Bank 2002). Second, rural employment, a basic precondition for broad-based growth, has increased more rapidly in Nicaragua with agro-exports. Agricultural exports are also relatively more labor intensive than import-competing agriculture. Exportables are less constrained in growth potential vis-à-vis production for the small Nicaraguan domestic market. Nicaragua is now more integrated into the world economy, so there is less protection for the production of importables (and more incentives to expand exports).

Most striking at this juncture is that the current prominent feature of Nicaragua's agriculture is its tradability vis-à-vis international markets. In spite of the small share of farmland devoted to the production of exportables (just 25 percent of harvested area), overall agricultural trade—the value of imports plus exports—represented 84 percent of agricultural GDP in 1998. This is above average, topping the figures for agricultural trade as a share of agricultural GDP in countries such as Costa Rica, Honduras and Ecuador. The high tradability of agriculture in Nicaragua implies that actions to increase access to foreign markets are crucial for the future of the sector.

Moreover, the performance of non-traditionals in Nicaragua's agriculture was the dynamic engine in the 1990s. Agricultural exports in Nicaragua account for more than half of total exports, of which coffee accounts for about a third. However, the *average* performance in exports conceals a significant difference between traditional exports and non-traditional exports. While traditional exports increased and then declined (rising from US$239 million in 1990 to $247 million in 1995, only to fall back to $225 million by 2000), non-traditional exports doubled and then quadrupled, albeit from a low base (rising steeply from US$19 million in 1990 to $33 million in 1995, and then on to US$85 million by 2000). By 2000, non-traditional agricultural products in Nicaragua already represented almost one-third of the sector's exports. There are four areas in which action is needed to improve the competitiveness of Nicaragua's agricultural sector:

▩ Supporting modernization of agribusiness
▩ Promoting agricultural exports
▩ Improving the effectiveness of public spending
▩ Strengthening public-private partnerships

Key issues in each of these areas are set out in the next four sections, after which a section entitled "A Roadmap for Increased Competitiveness in Agriculture" offers recommendations for action.

Supporting Modernization of Agribusinesses

The full positive impact of the openness to agricultural trade that began in Nicaragua in the early 1990s has not yet been realized. The reasons range from market inefficiencies and bottlenecks in agricultural services to substantial deficiencies in productive infrastructure. Thus, currently, domestic market imperfections and considerable implicit and explicit transaction costs favor import-competing activities, selling to the small Nicaraguan domestic market, at the expense of export production. The problems translate into huge limitations and undue costs to doing agribusiness in Nicaragua. They include: (i) market structures characterized by oligopolies and oligopsonies, as evidenced in inputs markets and agro-processing; (ii) inefficient and costly services to agriculture (packaging, quality control, phytosanitary tests, etc.); (iii) asymmetric information and lack of transparency of international prices; and (iv) inefficient and/or insufficient productive infrastructure, from roads and seaports to airports and telecommunications.

TABLE 8: REASONS FOR INADEQUACY/INCONSISTENCY OF PRODUCE QUALITY

Causes \1	Product					
	Peanut	Sesame	Soybean	Coffee	Fruit	Veg.
Shortcomings in the availability of certified genetic material	*	***	**		*	***
Lack of investments into farms due to high costs of capital and/or insecurity of land tenure		*	*	*	**	**
Shortcomings in the availability of production technology		*	*	**	**	**
Inadequate harvesting		*		**	*	*
Not use of quality standards to grade produces according to variety/origin/ organoleptic features/external appearance/ degree of damage etc			**	***	***	
Lack of post-harvest know-how/equipment/ facilities (excluding processing)		*			**	**
Technological shortcomings at processing level \2		**		***	\3	\3
Not use of adequate packaging materials and transport means towards final markets					***	***

\1 Relevance of the cause grows with the amount of * given;
\2 For coffee, the scoring refers to activities carried out at both wet mill and dry mill level;
\3 For fruit and vegetables, only the fresh produce was taken into consideration.
Source: Serpagli (2000).

Improving Agricultural Services and Increasing Chain Integration[10]

Enhancing product quality and sanitary/phytosanitary controls. There is little evidence of quality and sanitary management systems countrywide and, in general, product quality is low by international standards. The reasons for inadequacy in this area differ from sector to sector, as shown in Table 8.

Services to support a comprehensive Quality Measurement System (QMS), covering good agricultural practices (GAP), good management practices (GMP) and Hazardous Analyses of Critical Control Points (HACCP), are limited. When services are available, technical assistance is provided by either external partners (importers) or by projects financed by the donor's community. The reluctance of the private sector to step in to provide specialized services is explained by the low price differential in the domestic market in the case of fruit and vegetables and the undifferentiated external market in the case of coffee and sesame. Organic products (cocoa, coffee, sesame and vegetables) are an important exception. Two private companies provide certification services.

Official produce quality standards (as part of national QMS) apply only for limited products. Quality grading largely differs from the destination market, domestic or foreign. In this latter case, grading is either made compulsory by country's legislation (coffee), or by the recipient markets (sesame, peanuts, fruit and vegetables). In the domestic market, official quality standards currently exist only for green coffee, beans, potatoes and dried onions.

The country is poorly equipped to apply sanitary and phytosanitary controls in compliance with WTO guidelines (either US or EU). This translates into the inability to control levels of

---

10. Constraints in agricultural services have been identified in a recent in-depth study on coffee, fruit & vegetables, peanuts, soy and sesame seed. Although the analysis in this section is on the basis of these products, conclusions are representative of constraints for the export sector as a whole.

hazardous elements in exported products (for example, aflatoxin in peanuts and ocratoxin in coffee). Besides, criteria used by the various Ministries to accredit the structures (laboratories) for quality controls are controversial. While according to law N° 290 the Ministry of Development, Industry and Commerce (MIFIC) is responsible for the accreditation of all structures (laboratories) for quality controls, another law (291) assigns the same responsibility to MAGFOR when dealing with agricultural products.

Increasing access to market information systems (MISs). A large number of sources of agricultural market information are currently operated in Nicaragua. A key role in collecting and circulating market intelligence data is played by The Ministry of Agriculture, Livestock and Rural Development (MAGFOR), through its Information System on Agricultural Prices and Markets (SIPMA). However, this service faces major financial difficulties to will be hard put to continue its operations at current funding levels. Furthermore, despite the apparent abundance of market information, producers' organizations often complain of lacking the kind of information they need (Serpagli 2002). Producers report inadequate "availability of market information" as an important bottleneck constraining their domestic and foreign market performance. It appears that the market information that is available has a limited positive impact on domestic producers' market performance.

Integrating production chains. The low level of efficiency in domestic marketing of agricultural products is quite evident when marketing margins throughout the chain are calculated. The table below shows the margins for some selected products during the year 2000. The data clearly demonstrate the inefficient performance of the domestic agricultural marketing system. The lowest agricultural margin between producer and retailer (in the case of tomatoes) is 105 percent, while the highest (white cabbage) is 210 percent.

TABLE 9: MARKETING MARGINS FOR SELECTED AGRICULTURAL PRODUCTS

Product	Unit	Producer Level Price (C$) \2	Index	Wholesaler Level Price (C$) \2	Index	Retailer Level Price (C$) \2	Index
Soybean	QQ \1	130.41	100	205.57	158	298.00	229
White cabbage	Unit	1.57	100	3.70	236	4.87	310
Yellow Onion	QQ	147.00	100	314.45	214	415.00	282
Table Tomato	25 lbs.	53.22	100	90.12	169	109.25	205
Banana	250 units	21.83	100	48.95	224	66.25	303

\1 QQ= 100 pounds or 45,36 Kg
\2 Prices refer to national yearly averages.
Source: MAGFOR 2002.

Such variations in price are a direct result of several bottlenecks, including: (i) a lack of integration of the various components of the chain, which leads to an unduly high number of intermediaries playing a role in the marketing of agricultural outputs; (ii) a still-limited degree of producers' organization; (iii) a concentration of retail marketing of agricultural products in a few hands; (iv) a limited use of modern sales techniques and procedures, as opposed to traditional ones; (v) a high incidence of transport costs; and (vi) inadequate planning in the production of supplies.

Reduction of the current, high transaction costs in the marketing of agricultural products in Nicaragua will require a shortening of the marketing chain, a tightening of chain integration. That is a feasible task, particularly since it mainly needs to be applied only to export crops. As already shown in several examples of production chains, products sold for domestic consumption do not exhibit such high transaction costs or such lengthy marketing chains as do products destined for export. This applies in particular to horticultural products, due to the limited amount of operators who presently control the domestic marketing of these products. Producers should pursue a higher degree of control over the marketing of their horticultural harvests, by taking advantage, through the use of contracts, of the future nationwide enlargement of retailing systems other than the traditional ones (which make use of wholesale and retail markets).[11]

The use of modern sales procedures, as opposed to traditional ones, is still limited in most of the productive chains studied. There is a need to expand the use of contracts as an effective way to shorten marketing chains; to increase the use of more transparent and effective marketing facilities already operating in the country (such as BAGSA); and to introduce new facilities (such as electronic auctions for trading coffee).

Increasing Margins by Improving Productive Infrastructure

Despite considerable advances in the 1990s in targeted public spending on infrastructure, Nicaragua has considerable deficiencies in productive infrastructure that continue to hamper the competitiveness of Nicaraguan agricultural products in foreign markets. The country has made strides in telecommunications and electricity through privatization and attraction of foreign investment. However, serious bottlenecks remain in the roads network and port infrastructure. Similarly, important regions of the country that have significant productive potential are still confronted with seriously inadequate infrastructure. Overcoming such infrastructure bottlenecks will necessarily require private-sector participation. The public sector, mainly through its Ministry of Transport, will need to find new ways of attracting private-sector interest in investing in infrastructure and managing maintenance funds. One way may be to use using foreign aid for seed capital to attract private-sector investment.

Roads. The road network in Nicaragua has a limited outreach compared to other nations, ranking 55 among 62 countries in terms of kilometers per capita (Serpagli 2002). Only twenty-tree percent of the national road network is paved. Forty-eight percent of it cannot be used during the rainy season, as shown in the table below. The average speed of a truck that crosses the region is only 14 km/hour (given both the condition of roads and the delays at border crossings).

TABLE 10: ROAD NETWORK

Type of Road	Extent nationwide, as of 1999 (km)	Proportion of total network (%)
Paved highway	1,750	10.2
Paved road	2,150	12.5
All weather road	5,000	29.1
Dry season only road	8,275	48.2
Total road network	17,175	100.0

Source: CEI 2001.

Although no full, comprehensive technical assessment has been conducted to analyze the current bottlenecks in the road network and to identify the highest-priority areas for improvement, a rapid assessment carried out by Serpagli (2002) suggests the following priorities:

- Completion of the road linking the Pan-American Highway to Puerto Cabezas (main Nicaraguan port on the Atlantic coast). Currently, the road is reported to be in acceptable conditions to Rio Blanco, while east of this city, major investments are needed to complete paving of the 330 km. remaining;
- Repairs to the road linking Corinto Port to Chinandega, thus assuring a linkage to the primary road leading to Honduras. The main obstacle appears to be the rebuilding of the bridge

---

11. This, in particular, refers to distribution systems such as those implemented by multi-purpose retailers.

at Paso Caballos due to its estimated cost (about US$5 million, according to MTI). The National Port Enterprise ("Empresa Portuaria Nacional-EPN") intends to finance a technical study for the rebuilding of the bridge (Serpagli 2002).

▨ Completion of the road linking Muhan to El Rama (river port linking the South-Eastern part of Nicaragua to the Atlantic Ocean). Work was started early in 2002 (using WB funds) and estimated completion date is the end of 2003. Once completed, this road would allow the El Rama port to be linked to the Pan-American Highway; and

▨ Advancement in the development and maintenance of the secondary road system, linking villages and farms to primary roads. Lack in this area strongly limits the marketing of some crops (including coffee, fruits and vegetables) and hinders development of the country's Northwest.

Ports. Nicaragua has five seaports, three of which are located on the Pacific Coast (Corinto, Sandino and San Juan del Sur) and two on the Atlantic Coast (Puerto Cabezas and El Bluff). Nicaragua also has a river-port (El Rama). From 1997–2001, a series of major upgrading activities were implemented in all of the Nicaraguan seaports. To stimulate sea-transport companies to use Nicaraguan ports, the National Port Enterprise (EPN) implemented the following policy: (i) only loading/offloading services are charged for containers ("servicios al barco" are not charged, as it is done in all other Central American ports) and (ii) tariffs are negotiated on a "product-by-product" basis. This policy resulted in a 43 percent increase (from MT 1.55 million to MT 2.21 million) in the overall amount of goods handled at Nicaraguan seaports from 1996 to 2000.

There is a general consensus among local business community that: (i) the main port of Corinto, on the Pacific Coast is ill-placed to serve EU and U.S. (East Coast) destinations, and (ii) the lack of a deep-water harbor on the Atlantic Coast and the current state of port infrastructure and management put Nicaragua at a disadvantage in the development of a competitive export business, when compared to neighboring countries (Costa Rica and Honduras, both of which have good port infrastructure on the Atlantic Coast).

From September 2001 to October 2002, 66 percent of the total country's coffee exports were shipped from Puerto Cortez (Honduras), while only about 32 percent from Puerto Corinto (Nicaragua) (IDB 2001). The use of foreign ports is reflected in the substantial difference between the CIF price in New York and the FOB price in Matagalpa (one of the main coffee-producing areas in the country), caused mainly by the transport cost. A second factor is that the cost of transport by land from Matagalpa to Puerto Cortez of a container of about MT 17 (US$1,200) equals the sea freight cost of the same container from Puerto Cortez to New York. It is then fair to say that coffee exports from Nicaragua are heavily penalized (when compared to exports from Honduras and Costa Rica) due to the lack of adequate port facilities on the Atlantic coast.

The current port situation is likely to improve soon as a result of recent investments in port infrastructures, changes in port management, and adjustments in the provision of port services (following the transfer of ports' management—as a whole, in the case of Puerto Cabezas, or in part, in the case of the other Nicaraguan ports—through privatization). The Government also has plans to further complete and restructure the Puerto Cabezas harbor's facility and the road system connecting the Pan-American Highway to both Puerto Cabezas and Puerto Corinto. In the interim, measures to stimulate use of the Nicaragua's main ports should be conceived along with the implementation of publicity campaigns to inform the local business community about progress made in upgrading the quality of the ports' infrastructure and services.

Electricity. Major differences exist between rural and urban areas in access to electricity, as shown in the table below. In Managua, the Pacific and Central regions, the percentage of the population having access to electricity ranges from 56 percent to 68 percent of the total population, while the least developed regions (the Atlantic and the North ones) show much lower levels. These averages have not increased much during the last ten years. As a result, more than half of the country's population did not have access to electricity as at the end of 1999 (INCAE 2002).

Limited access to electricity is a major constraint in the use of processing facilities (for coffee at wet mill level), modern communication (fax and internet) and production equipment (pumping of water into irrigation systems is reported to be dependent upon availability of electricity in Nicaragua).

TABLE 11: ACCESS TO ELECTRICITY IN NICARAGUA		
	Population with access/Total population (%)	
Region	1990	1999
North	28	36
Pacific	53	56
Managua	68	68
Central	42	57
Atlantic	9	17
National	45	49

Source: INCAE 2001.

Electricity used for agricultural purposes does not pay 15 percent VAT. As a result, the yearly average cost of electricity for pumping and irrigation (US$85.4/kwh and US$82.5/kwh respectively in 2001) is lower than any other use (BCN 2002).[12] In 2001, the demand for irrigation and pumping purposes totaled 5.8 percent and 10.0 percent respectively of the country's total electricity consumption (BCN 2002).

A proposal to link up all Central American countries with just one power network (called SIEPAC) has been recently introduced by the Latin American Energy Organization (OLADE) and is in the process of being reviewed by the various Governments in the region. It is also worth noting, that in 1998, the electricity generated through natural processes (geothermic) was 5.8 percent of the total domestic production 13 and that in 2001 the private sector contributed to the production of 57 percent of electricity generated inside the country (BCN 2002).

As in the case of roads, expansion and upgrading of the domestic power network should remain a long-term priority for government authorities, given the consequences, for the production of agricultural products, processing and marketing, of insufficient and inconsistent electricity access.

Telecommunications. Despite progress made in the 1990s, much remains to be done in Nicaragua to expand telecommunications coverage, particularly in less developed regions of the country, where the available number of telephone lines remains extremely low. Still, the following table shows the significant progress made over the past decade.

Promoting Agricultural Exports

An analysis of the competitiveness of Nicaragua's main crops provides important guidance for trade policy. Nicaragua has already achieved good levels of trade liberalization, but this trend toward openness will need to continue. The country's agricultural growth will require a shifting of incentives to support production of non-traditional crops for export.

The analysis of the cost structure for rice and beans indicates that in fact both of these crops are internationally competitive. By contrast, the analysis of the cost structure of maize, together with

---

12. While irrigation water is exclusively for agricultural uses, pumped water can be used also for industrial or other purposes.

13. Since July 1999, the geothermic Momotombo Plant entered into a joint-venture with the Israeli firm ORMAT. In 1998, the Momotombo Plant produced 5.8 percent of the whole amount of electricity produced in Nicaragua.

TABLE 12: ACCESS TO TELEPHONE SERVICE IN NICARAGUA (1990, 1999)

Region	Number of telephone lines/1000 inhabitants	
	1990	1999
North	4.0	30.4
Pacific	10.3	13.1
Managua	29.4	22.0
Central	6.5	73.7
Atlantic	0.9	20.3
National	12.1	30.4

Source: INCAE 2001.

sorghum and sugar cane, indicates that these three crops are not competitive vis-à-vis international markets. They exhibit lower border prices than domestic prices. [14]

However, maize has certain peculiarities that set it apart. First, tariffs for maize are low (10 percent) if compared with sorghum and sugar cane (30 percent and 55 percent respectively). Second, for maize production Nicaragua is self-sufficient with marginal levels of exports. Maize is practically a non-tradable, with about 141,000 farms (or 71 percent of all farms) producing white maize for human consumption. Given the tariff level, the high Nominal Protection Rate (NPR) exhibited for maize is derived from high transaction costs along the trade chain. That is, market inefficiencies. Thus, trade policies that lower general tariff levels will tend not to have a significant negative impact on small producers. On the contrary, they could favor lower consumer prices for staple food.

Does openness to trade pose a risk of increased polarization in agriculture? In other words, is there a risk of substantial dynamic growth among a subset of commercially oriented farmers, and a lack of dynamism among those less prepared to take advantage of the economic liberalization arising from economic reforms? Market reforms including trade liberalization are likely to have a differentiated impact in agriculture. The experience in several countries in Latin America suggests that the impact differed between import-competing and exportables, geographic regions, farm sizes, and sub-periods (Foster and Váldes 2001). The import-competing sector, and particularly small farmers within this sub-sector, is the group with the most visible problems. Although it is tempting to press for higher border protection to deal with small farmers income problems, arguing their lack of flexibility to switch to different cropping patterns, higher protection is not the only income policy option. Quite the opposite, in the long run it may prove to be a counterproductive route. Alternative routes to assist this sub-sector include targeted programs aimed at improvements in roads, further developments in the financial sector, targeted (temporary) income transfers (for example, ProCampo in Mexico), agricultural research and technology transfers, and initiatives to promote non-farm employment opportunities in rural areas. In fact, current government efforts to re-address IDR priorities towards productive support to farmers in dynamic areas is a step in the right direction.

Improving Effectiveness of Public Spending

Severe institutional problems are currently undermining the critical role and potential impact of public expenditure on production incentives and competitiveness in agriculture, as well as the delivery of public goods and services in rural areas. Both government and foreign aid expenditures

---

14. The methodology used to analyze the competitiveness of the selected crops compared the boarder price of each crop, adjusted to reflect the cost at farm-gate, with the domestic cost at farm-gate. To adjust the border price to reflect the cost at farm-gate, for each crop we subtracted from the boarder price the costs that would be incurred if the crop were to be moved from farm-gate to the boarder (that is, using the same values of the nominal rates of protection).

TABLE 13: SELECTED INDICATORS TO ESTIMATE CROP COMPETITIVENESS (2001)

Crops	Number of farms (thousands)	% of total farms	% farms > 10 mz.	Weight in		Border Price* (US$/QQ)	Unit Cost* (US$/QQ)	Current Tariff (%)
				GDP	Agr. GDP			
Importables								
Maize	141.4	70.9	32	3.4	14.1	5.13	5.59	10
Rice	17.3	8.7	25	2.8	7.4	10.74	8.34	62**
Irrigation	0.3	0.2	15	nd	nd	10.74	8.69	62**
Rain-fed	17.0	8.5	25	nd	nd	10.74	7.99	62**
Sorghum	2.5	1.3	34	0.4	1.3	5.22	5.60	30
Exportables								
Coffee	43.2	21.6	34	6.2	22.0	22.57	21.23	15
Sugar Cane	6.5	3.3	20	1.9	6.7	27.00	31.30	55
Peanuts	0.1	0.1		0.5	1.9	14.84	11.94	5
Beans	115	57.6	32	2.2	8.8	14.25	10.50	10
Sesame***	4	2.0	100	0.1	0.4	32.50	23.70	5
Meat	97	48.6	13	4.0	15.0	0.88	0.73	15

*At farm-gate price
**Tariff for Rice was currently raised to 85 percent. Calculations are however based on the previous value of 62 percent.
***A different methodology was used for sesame due to lack of accurate available data. This estimates are based on international prices rather than border prices.
Source: PROVIA 2002

in rural areas have been substantial, but they have not been cost-effective. Their high variability from year-to-year in quantity and focus has undermined implementation. Such expenditure, if effective, would be key to promoting rapid growth and reducing rural poverty. In many cases, serious institutional problems have only been worsened by heavy dependence on external financing.

As for the inflow of public resources, government expenditures in rural areas unfortunately have been erratic and ineffective (World Bank 2001). Public spending on agriculture represents a relatively small and highly variable component of total public spending, despite the priority given to rural development in Nicaragua's Poverty Reduction Strategy Paper. Nevertheless, in absolute terms, substantial sums have been spent on agriculture and on rural development, mainly under the rubric of capital spending, mostly grant-financed from external sources. Capital spending on agriculture in the 1990s grew, but erratically. Current and capital expenditures grew from 2.6 percent of Central Government Expenditures in 1991 to 8.4 percent in 2001, or from 0.7 percent of GDP to 2.3 percent respectively. These ratios are small relative to the agricultural sector's substantial 30 percent contribution to GDP. In absolute terms, public spending rose significantly from about US$11 million in 1991 to $79 million in 2001 (World Bank 2001).

The Nicaraguan experience with public expenditure aimed at assisting the agricultural sector and rural areas, as analyzed by the World Bank (2001), indicates that a wide variety of public programs have been promoted, ranging from institutional strengthening, agricultural technology, agricultural sanitary and protection services and food distribution to food-for-work programs, irrigation and marketing of basic grains. However, these programs have not been well coordinated and can even provide conflicting signals and incentives to various economic agents. Lacking systematic monitoring and evaluation data, it is difficult to evaluate past programs. Relevant for rural areas, though still preliminary, the "Review of Selected Poverty Programs in Nicaragua's PRSP Portfolio" (draft May 18, 2001) describes a mixed picture of the performance of past programs. Some 30 percent of

BOX 2:   ESTIMATION OF NOMINAL AND EFFECTIVE PROTECTION RATES FOR
         AGRICULTURE IN NICARAGUA

Analysis of competitiveness is substantiated by the estimation of nominal and effective rates of protection (NPR
and EPR, respectively) elaborated by PROVIA (2001). Shown in the table below, these indicators show protection profiles for both importables and exportables, computed both at prevailing rates (nominal rates) and at
parity exchange rates (effective rates).

Product	1996/1997		1998/1999		2000/2001		2001/2002	
	Nominal	Effective	Nominal	Effective	Nominal	Effective	Nominal	Effective
Importables								
Maize	32	35	84	95	54	67	35	37
Rice	87	85	29	45	40	57	44	82
Sorghum	9	22	50	103	61	119	26	46
Soybean	-4	-5	15	26	27	39	0	-1
Exportables								
Coffee	-1	0	0	1	0	1	2	3
Sugar Cane	-11	-8	-4	-19	-7	-9	-1	-18
Peanut	11	18	1	3	1	1	1	2
Beans	0	1	1	1	1	1	1	2
Sesame	-1	2	1	2	-2	-2	-2	-4
Meat	0	0	1	2	1	1	1	2

Source: PROVIA 2001.

These figures confirm that consumers of maize, sorghum and rice are paying higher domestic prices as compared to the import parity price. For importables, maize, rice and sorghum production have benefited from
comparatively higher rates of nominal protection. Effective rates are still higher. By contrast, farm prices for
exportables are closer to the corresponding border prices at both nominal and effective rate estimations.

A decomposition analysis of NPR and EPR (PROVIA 2001) also confirms that market imperfections are mostly
responsible for raising the value domestic value added for both importables and exportables. Structural inefficiencies, market segmentation, and costly services to agriculture translate into an implicit tax on exports.

As a measure to revert the anti-export bias the government should aim at establishing lower and unified tariffs
over time for all crops, allowing enough time for producers to adjust and make their transition to higher value
crops or other more productive activities, urban or rural. This is likely to trigger the resistance of producer
organizations and lobby groups. A well-designed, concerted strategy will be needed to balance the economic
gains with the political costs.

programs do address a specific risk and seem to reach the poor, but the effectiveness of the remaining 70 percent is dubious. Roughly 45 percent have design problems but there is insufficient information to make a solid assessment. Another 25 percent do not address specific risks of the rural
poor. Among these are many projects to improve household incomes through rural development.
The operational efficiency of many projects was questionable, in part due to inadequate design (having required unrealistic financial and managerial capacity among the poor), as well as duplication
and fragmentation of activities. Projects in health and education were found to be more consistent
with sector policies, but those in rural development, housing and disaster response seemed to be ad
hoc. Overall, projects funded were donor-driven rather than target-group driven. The erratic nature
of funding—the annual variation in funding varied from plus 157 percent to minus 32 percent—
undermined proper planning and efficient implementation.

Another ongoing study of the projects funded by public spending in agriculture finds that a combination of project dispersion and high administrative costs has rendered many projects virtually ineffective (SETEC 2002). The study also finds that such problems arise in part from the lack of sufficient intervention by government agencies (due largely to institutional weaknesses) to define, coordinate and execute the numerous projects financed by donors.

As shown in the Table 14, estimates of the amounts of public resources dedicated to the agricultural sector indicate that a substantial rise occurred in the second half of the 1990s. Support to the sector coming from price support (non-monetary) plus actual public spending (excluding rural infrastructure and rural integrated projects) went from 7 to around 13 percent as a share of gross agricultural product between 1996 and 2000. Through the same period, the relative structure of support to the agricultural sector changed: price support more than doubled from 31 to 65 percent of total support; consistent with the increasing use of tariff instruments. Thus, the relative share of public-sector support that came in the form of actual public spending went down from 51 to 30 percent. Still, the absolute amount of public expenditures rose substantially during the period, by about 25 percent. Much of the rise was related to extraordinary expenditures after Hurricane Mitch. Meanwhile, there was a rise in the use of price supports, through tariffs, as a way of protecting producers of importables from low international commodity prices.

Since the Government's strategy envisages the private sector as the lead agent in promoting faster growth, decreases in price support (lowering of tariffs) may not necessarily require increases in the level of public spending. In order to increase the efficiency and effectiveness of future expenditures in agriculture, the government needs to make public spending more focused and linked with overall export-oriented and competitiveness objectives.

Strengthening Public-Private Partnerships

Any strategy to improve the sector competitiveness has a crucial pre-condition: to establish and strengthen successful partnerships among policy-makers and the domestic and foreign private sector. Increasingly, leaders are seeing the functions that might have been viewed as clearly the government's domain also require attention from the business (Austin 2000). The underlying logic for establishing partnerships is that both the public and the private sector have unique characteristics that provide them with advantages in specific aspects of services or project delivery. The most successful partnership arrangements draw on the strengths of both the public and private sector to establish complementary relationship (PPP 1999). While the individual actors—government, and private sector may be effective in achieving their specific goals, no one can solve every issue of common concern.

TABLE 14: SUPPORT TO THE AGRICULTURAL SECTOR

Concepts	Current C$ (millions)				Constant 1994 C$ (millions)	
	1996	%	2000	%	1996	2000
I. Support to producers	142.4	49.1	673.3	70.3	115.1	354.9
A. Price support (via protection/non-monetary)	89.3	30.8	625.2	65.3	72.2	329.6
B. Waiving of tariffs on agricultural inputs	53.1	18.3	48.1	5.0	42.9	25.4
II. Support through public exp. in agriculture*	147.4	50.9	284.1	29.7	119.1	149.8
III. Estimation of total support	289.8	100.0	957.4	100.0	234.2	504.7
IV. Gross agricultural product	4069.8		7401.0		3287.4	3901.3
V. Coeffcient of support to agriculture	7.1		12.9		7.1	12.9

*excludes infrastructure and rural integrated projects
Source: PROVIA, 2002.

Collaboration and coordination among the two actors can lead to the production of some essential collective goods and services still not provided by individual actor (Linder 2000).

In fact, there are three main reasons for establishing PPP supporting rural development. First, successful partnerships between the public and the private sector create an enabling environment for the macro-sectoral economic policy. Private sector participation helps remove biases in economic policies against exports and agriculture, encourages the implementation of anti-monopoly measures to increase the competitive structure of the economy, and promotes active policy measures for cost-effective and efficient human resources development.

Second, successful partnerships between the public and the private sector share the costs and the risks of joint projects. Such co-operation can produce far greater benefits for both partners and for the country than a purely public or private sector investment. Public funds are used to mobilize and leverage private sector investments. Development co-operation can thus become cheaper, more efficient and more sustainable in areas such as harvest, processing, packing, storage and shipment. The Public-Private Partnership seems also to be a promising sustainable way to strengthen agricultural research, and provide new technologies to the resource-poor farmers.

Third, successful partnerships between the public and the private sector can help to ensure the integration of the private sector's new role in social processes. The power of partnership comes from their participative and multi-stakeholder nature. A partnership based on the premise that all stakeholders in development issue should mobilize to develop and implement plans to address the issue (Leisinger 2000).

Therefore, tri-lateral partnerships involving private companies, civil society and the state are a promising foundation for sustainable and structurally effective measures. The commonly recognized concept of Corporate Social Responsibility (CSR) can serve as a stimulator for such partnerships. CSR is the continuing commitment by business to behave ethically and contribute to economic development while improving the quality of life of the workforce and their families as well as of the local community and society at large.[15] In political science terms, CSR includes: a) a company running its business responsibly in relation to internal stakeholders; b) its role in relationship to the state, locally and nationally, as well as to inter-state institutions or standards; and c) its role as a responsible member of the society in which it operates and the global community. The first role involves the companies' core business in relation to its internal stakeholders (shareholders, management, employees, customers and suppliers). This includes ensuring its own house is in order, corporate governance, product responsibility, employment conditions, workers rights, training and education. The second role includes abiding by relevant legislation, and the company's responsibility as a tax payer, ensuring that the state can function effectively. A company's third role, as a member of society, is also multi-layered. This involves the company's relations with the people and environment in the communities in which it operates and those to which it exports. Too often, CSR at this level is understood as a transfer of financial resources from business to a worthy activity, but a financial contribution alone fails to take advantage of the most valuable contributions that a company has to make. This third role lends itself well to partnership arrangements: voluntary, multi-sectoral, consensual, based on shared objectives and the notion of 'core complementary competencies', with each party providing resources that derive from their core activities and that are complementary to those provided by the other actors, resulting in synergistic improvements to outcomes (Reyes 2002).

When private enterprises, supported by other stakeholders, establish operations based on their social and environmental responsibility they tend to have a significant and long-term positive impact on local economies. The benefits for the community can be summarized using the following categories: a) job creation, b) cut down on the black market due to improved access to goods and services, c) training, education, and skills enhancement, d) addressing the issue of child labor,

---

15. The above definition of CSR was developed in 1998 by WBCSD For further information, please visit: http://www.wbcsd.org/newscenter/reports/2000/CSR2000Making%20Good%20Business%20Sense.pdf

---

BOX 3: CSR - STARBUCKS COMMITMENT TO ORIGINS, FAIR TRADE AND FARM DIRECT

One of Starbucks initiatives is partnership with Conservation International. Together they are working with coffee producers to promote coffee cultivation methods that protect biodiversity and improve livelihood of coffee farmers. Growing coffee in the environment provided traditional production regimes can result in higher quality, better tasting beans that have more value in the world coffee market. This, in turn, can lead to increased income of small farmers. In 2000 Starbucks introduced jointly with Trans Fair USA "Fair Trade Certification"—a system that seeks to improve the lives of coffee growers in origin countries by ensuring that the owners of small family farmers receive a guaranteed price for their harvest. Fair Trade certification provides a way for these farmers to increase their incomes by helping them organize into cooperatives and linking them directly to coffee importers and roasters. Fair Trade also encourages buyers to extend financial credit to farmer cooperatives and develop long-term relationships. Another initiative is "Farm Direct." Coffee is purchased directly from producers under long-term contracts. In the end, both parties benefit from this process. Starbucks is assured of a quality product, and the farmer receive a guaranteed price for his coffee for several years.

Source: Starbucks, 2001.[16]

e) gender equality, f) housing, g) health care, g) community development, h) higher minimum wage, and i) better work place conditions. At the same time the impact of CSR on enterprise competitiveness can be unbundled in five overlapping elements: a) enhancing reputation and brands, b) more efficient operations, c) improved financial performance, d) increased sales and consumer loyalty, and e) increased ability to attract and retain quality employees (World Bank Institute 2001).

However, despite the fact that the differences actors are the source of the strength of partnerships, they are also the source of particular challenges. Bringing together actors with diverse goals, values and perspectives means there is plenty of ground for misunderstandings and conflicts. Therefore, creating partnerships requires building structures, skills, and processes that can use the differences to encourage exchange and creativity. Effective partnership building process must involve, two way communication between interested actors (Grayson 2002). Members of partnership can benefit from partnering by being able to: a) increase the scale of their activities, b) raise their credibility, c) take advantage of each partner's strength, d) mobilize resources and exchange of information, e) reduce transaction costs and risks, f) create new ideas and solutions to common problems, and g) achieve a mutual goal that would be unattainable if each actor were working alone (Leisinger 2000).

A Roadmap for Increased Competitiveness in Agriculture

Following is a list of recommendations aimed at boosting the international competitiveness of Nicaragua's agricultural sector by addressing key issues and bottlenecks identified in preceding sections. The recommendations are grouped here in descending order of priority, in four main fronts: (i) Supporting modernization of agribusiness, (ii) Promoting exports, (iii) Improving the effectiveness of public spending, and (iv) Strengthening public-private partnerships.

Addressed to the government, the Roadmap provides a basis for discussion between the public sector, the private sector, and the donors' community on how to set the priority-agenda for a shared, competitiveness strategy. To address the risks of increasing polarization within the agricultural sector, a worsening of the already dualistic structure of Nicaragua's agriculture production, the government may want to: (i) Seek consensus with major stakeholders on the best design and sequence of reforms, explicitly taking into consideration the trade-offs involved in alternative

---

16. for more visit Starbucks web site at http://www.starbucks.com/aboutus/CSR_FY01_AR.pdf

approaches, with attention to the needs of producers of highly protected crops and poor producers of importables; and (ii) Seek agreement with the donor community on how best to support the poor through programs of productive support as well as food security.

First Priority Front: Supporting Modernization of Agribusinesses
Key Recommendation:
Enlarge and upgrade domestic transport and utilities infrastructure. The current market imperfections and the considerable implicit and explicit transaction costs can be greatly reduced by targeted policies and investments to improve transport and utilities infrastructure. First, government should focus on upgrading domestic power networks by stimulating the private sector to increase its current share of energy generation. ENEL should revise its electrical tariffs for agricultural uses to make them more easy to understand for producers, and consider the possibility of making them more affordable through transitional subsidies. Second, MIFIC and MINEX should work together in developing a strategy to attract sea-carrier companies based on incentives and improved port services. EPN should continue current efforts to improve seaports, including exploring the possibility of developing a seaport on the Atlantic coast. MAGFOR and MIFIC in coordination with EPN should run effective awareness campaigns to stimulate use of domestic port facilities and services among the domestic business community. Third, investments should be made as to complete the road linking the Pan-American Highway to Puerto Cabezas, to repair the road linking Corinto Port to Chinandega, to complete the road linking Muhan to El Rama, and to advance the development and maintenance of the secondary road system, linking villages and farms to primary roads. Direct involvement of local authorities ("Alcaldías") in these plans will greatly assure the correct road maintenance and access to eligible funds (for example, IDR and INIFOM/ FONDEM, among others).

Other Recommendations:
Rationalize production processes, by: (i) Promoting a shift in the extension services offered by INTA, IDR and FUNICA towards a common, shared research and extension agenda, aimed at boosting competitiveness by providing not only technical but also economic and marketing know-how. This would not require using more resources, but rather using resources more effectively; and (ii) Developing and financing strategies, through INTA, to support the production and use of genetically-improved seeds, as well as development of new varieties based on market demand and economic/ financial assessments.

Increase the quality of products and the use of quality and hygienic management systems by: (i) Developing and promoting (and possibly enforcing) the use of quality and hygienic management systems and norms, according to international standards (ISO, GAP, GMP, HACCP, grades and standards etc) and in compliance with WTO guidelines; and (ii) Promoting, by MAGFOR and INTA together with private input suppliers, the use of reliable seeds, skilled technical, economic and marketing assistance (post-harvest and sales/export) and greater standardization of produce (based on area of origin, altitude, variety, physical and organoleptic features, etc.)

Improve coverage and impact of existing Market Information Systems (MISs) by continuing to support MAGFOR-SIPMA's services, co-coordinating activities of MISs operated at the national level, and identifying targets to be achieved by the various MISs through national needs-assessment analyses.

Increase use of sales procedures alternatives by: (i) Developing and enforcing, in MIFIC, the use of tools (such as produce-grading systems) to allow trade to be based on clearly defined grades and standards; (ii) Strengthening, institutionally and managerially, the existing trading facilities (such as BAGSA), so they can deal proficiently with products not yet being traded (such as commercial coffee), (iii) Promoting the introduction of new trading facilities (e-commerce, electronic sub-auctions, auctions); and (iv) Running educational campaigns to teach operators how to use the new facilities, along with awareness campaigns to promote the use of both existing facilities (BAGSA) or new facilities to be established.

Second Priority Front: Promoting Agricultural Exports

Key Recommendation:

Create incentives for exports. Government can play a determinant role in promoting agricultural exports. First, it should promote a series of policy measures to create the right environment. These policy measures would have political implications, and should be negotiated openly with the private sector. They would include abstention from direct price controls in inputs and final products and the reduction/leveling of tariffs over time, to allow the government to engage in a process of lowering transaction costs (as is already being accomplished on other fronts, such as economic infrastructure, energy and financial services), and to allow producers to adjust their production patterns to new market signals. Second, government will need to creatively invest in direct incentives to support producers to stimulate successful transition to higher value-added activities. Examples of these incentives are the competitive funds for research, technical assistance, market studies, business plans preparation, etc. Direct transfers to farmers is not an option for Nicaragua, and it should be considered only as a measure of last resort.

Other Recommendations:

Encourage foreign direct investment in agriculture and agro-processing by: (i) adopting foreign investment laws and regulations that are transparent and applied equally to all; (ii) guaranteeing the repatriation of profits and capital at market exchange rates; and (iii) devising mechanisms for rapid and fair resolution of disputes.

  Eliminate current constraints on MIFIC's ability to pursue Nicaragua's interests in international, regional or bilateral negotiations. This would require financial provisions for staff to take part in meetings outside the country, along with provision of technical assistance and training for staff (perhaps from the donor community) on specific technical or legal matters under negotiation (such as country quotas for exporting peanuts into the U.S. market). MAGFOR and MIFIC need to implement consistent institutional efforts to protect domestic producers from unfair trading practices by other Central American (and any other) countries, such as dumping, product triangulation, etc.

  Promote a Common Tariffs System within Central America to eliminate non-tariff barriers that currently restrain free trade among neighboring countries.

  Increase efficiency of export-promotion incentive programs (such as the "Reintegro Tributario"). This may involve legally requiring quicker reimbursement times, for example, or improvement in targeting eligible operators. The effectiveness of export promotion services (such as those provided by CETREX) could also be improved by further reducing the number of documents required for export operations and eliminating needless duplication of certificates when the same operator is involved.

  Improve institutional effectiveness at the Customs Service level, to give preferential border crossing for perishable goods, for example. Generally, customs practices should be simplified to avoid delays in produce inspections (at dry-mill level in the case of coffee) and in the transfer of export documentation from central offices to the border post (as when exporting coffee to Honduras, for example).

Third Priority Front: Improving Effectiveness of Public Spending in Agriculture

Key Recommendation:

Coordinate effectively the use of donor resources. Relative to the size of its population, Nicaragua is one of the countries with higher donors' contributions for public spending for the rural sector in in the world. Yet, there is a wide recognition that lack of focus, variability over time and space, and ever-changing agendas strongly affected the effectiveness of these investments in the last decade. For the purpose of promoting agricultural exports, government should make a serious effort to coordinate financial aid within a clearly defined, broadly discussed agricultural competitiveness agenda. Moreover, it should develop specific indicators to measure the effectiveness of an export-promotion and broad-based growth strategy in agriculture. This can help guide all active agents in the sector, establishing investment priorities, particularly for donors who finance most of the capital budget. Strengthening the delivery mechanism of the Rural Development Institute (IDR, the key institution in charge of providing specialized, transitional support in the form of productive investments for small farmers) is possibly the single, most important measure in the short term. IDR should support a portfolio of programs carefully targeted to help small producers raise their productivity and management capacity. Criteria should be aimed at securing higher returns to public investments and encouraging profitability of sub-projects. Managing few sectoral programs with narrow, well-targeted productive objectives might prove to be much more effective than the current practice. The government and the donor community have an excellent opportunity to support the IDR in this direction at a moment when major rural development programs are about to be refinanced with IDB, European Union, IFAD, FAO and bilateral donors. Recent discussions with IDR officials suggest the institution is already working in this direction, but the government needs to promote a more proactive role. Decisive action here will help gain the confidence of the donor community, encouraging donors to support such transition programs.

Other Recommendations:
Aim public spending at improving social protection and rasing human capital among rural households. As discussed at length in Nicaragua's PRSP, investment in human capital will be essential if the idle part of Nicaragua's rural labor force is to become employed in either farm or non-farm work.

Improve the poverty focus of public productive investments. The social protection programs addressing the main risks and hardships facing the extreme poor will need to be complemented by support in productive investments and food security. INTA, FISE, MED have already developed relevant experience in these areas, which might prove useful in addressing the productive constraints of the poor.

Improve the poverty focus of public expenditures. This would also involve classifying which expenditures actually target the poor, and which aim at reducing poverty indirectly by promoting faster growth and employment.

Improve program efficiency by defining duration of assistance and criteria by which beneficiaries "graduate" from programs, by discontinuing or privatizing public programs that provide private services and constitute unfair competition with private suppliers of similar services.

Fourth Priority Front: Strengthening Public-Private Partnerships
Key Recommendation:
Define key roles to be played by the public and private sectors in promoting competitiveness and removing constraints for exports. Jointly, public and private sectors have key roles in promoting competitiveness and removing constraints for exports. The public sector has a crucial role in providing public goods, such as eliminating distortionary signals, providing infrastructure and facilitating information (such as market information). The private sector, domestic and foreign, needs to take the lead in identifying opportunities, facilitating the adoption of appropriate technologies, and making financial and marketing arrangements. Match makers, such as individuals or firms with knowledge about local conditions and links with domestic and foreign investors, can also have a role in identifying opportunities and helping match domestic and foreign firms with producers. Important international lessons can be drawn form the on-going efforts in many countries to boost Corporate Social Responsibility (CSR).

Other Recommendations:
Support organizational capacity of local organizations and associations in adding value to exports. Several activities are necessarily linked for improvements in quality, financing and marketing arrangements, and post-harvest practices to take place. Most producers organizations require institutional support and training to become effective partners in areas such as managerial and accounting capacity, and internal legitimacy. Producers and trade organizations can benefit from initial public sector support on successful experiences. Associations can gradually take over some processes and provide necessary linkages to domestic and foreign markets. They can become a good vehicle for transmitting rewards to farmers who deliver better quality (Cup of Excellence) and to establish successful vertical integration partnerships.

Establish a multi-stakeholder dialogue supporting competitiveness in rural sector through CSR practices. There is strong international evidence that establishing a permanent dialogue between corporations, governments, and civil society (stakeholders in business development) on the social and environmental responsibilities of the private sector (CSR) creates better conditions for economic competitiveness, improves employees' rights recognition, and minimizes the negative impact on the environment, thus overall increasing the standards of living of citizens. However, designing, facilitating and implementing multi-stakeholder dialogue requires developing special managerial skills, and building sustainable relationships among the stakeholders in a business activity. It has also to involve a genuine willingness on the part of the business sector and civil society to listen and learn from their contacts with each other. This development process itself requires investment of time and resources and a willingness to err and correct mistakes as part of a "learning-by-doing" process.

Of Crisis and Opportunity in the Coffee Sector: An Example of the Application of the Roadmap

Nicaraguan coffee producers stand at a crossroads. Their situation could be seen as an extreme, advanced version of what is already beginning to occur throughout the entire agricultural sector as globalization advances. World markets bring competitive pressures to bear and make it impossible to sustain inefficient production; but they also offer vast sources of demand which, when tapped successfully, can drive increased business and economic growth, and ultimately can contribute to significant poverty reduction.

The Crisis: International Competition and Low International Prices

Until the past two years, Nicaraguan coffee production was an important engine driving economic activity in the country. On average, between 1994 and 1999, coffee contributed US$140 million to the economy, representing some 5.3 percent of GDP. By the end of the 1990s, coffee was generating employment for 280,000 workers, or 42 percent of the rural labor force. In the 1999/2000 crop year 90 percent of farmers were small producers, harvesting less than 100 quintals/year. Collectively these small producers supplied 14percent of total Nicaraguan coffee production. The top 0.6 percent of Nicaraguan coffee producers were large-scale, harvesting over 1,500 quintals/year, and they supplied 36 percent of the country's total coffee production. Several indicators of growth rose dramatically over the decade from 1990 to 2001: yields improved by 40 percent, annual production volume rose by 93.1 percent from 932,000 quintals to 1,800,000 quintals, and annual export volume rose 115 percent from 849,000 quintals to 1,826,000.

However, during this same period, the world coffee market underwent significant changes, culminating in the steep drop in coffee prices over the past two years. Persistent global over-production and stagnant consumption have led to an accumulation of inventories, and competition has intensified between different sources. At the same time, there has been a substantial rise in price differentials for specialty coffees. Yet, overall prices have fallen sharply as new low-cost producers in Asia, such as Vietnam and Indonesia, have expanded production.

The drop in coffee prices below the costs of production in many places has caused hardship for coffee producers worldwide. The consequences for Nicaragua have been severe. Coffee export revenue dropped about 50 percent, from US$170 million in 2000/01 to US$85 million in 2001/02, causing great hardship in both economic and social terms. Nicaragua's balance of payment deficit has swollen to 38 percent. Employment has fallen dramatically, with permanent employment in coffee-production across Central America decreasing in 2001 by an estimated 54 percent from the year before, while seasonal employment fell an estimated 21 percent.

The Opportunity: Production Cost and Quality

Nicaragua already has some comparative advantage over other coffee-producing countries in terms of production costs, but in order to exploit this advantage, better marketing and promotion would be needed, as well as more consistency in quality. In turn, Nicaragua has the potential to develop comparative advantage in quality, because an unusually high proportion of its growing areas are at high altitudes, but in order to exploit this potential, production and post-harvesting practices must be improved and systems to ensure consistent high quality must be adopted.

Concerning cost: Among the 22 main coffee producing countries considered in the LMC report "Coffee in Crisis" (2002), Nicaragua and Honduras rank among the lowest-cost producers (though Vietnam is lowest, followed by Indonesia). Guatemala ranks among middle-cost producers, while Costa Rica and El Salvador are among the highest cost producers. The following table shows the LMC cost estimates for Central American countries, along with estimates by CEPAL which are slightly different but not far off.

TABLE 15: COFFEE PRODUCTION COST ESTIMATES		
Country	**LMC** **US$/quintal**	**CEPAL** **US$/quintal**
Costa Rica	100	86
El Salvador	84	57
Guatemala	74	74
Nicaragua	67	70
Honduras	65	70

Sources: CEPAL (2002, p.30), and the LMC report "Coffee in Crisis," 2002.

Concerning quality: Most coffee in Central America is classified as hard bean (HB), which grows at altitudes between 800 and 1,200 meters, and strictly hard bean (SHB), which grows at altitudes above 1,200 meters. These coffees, particularly the SHB varieties, often command significant premiums in the market. The table below shows, for each Central American country, the share of coffee production that comes from high altitudes. By far, the highest share of production classified as strictly hard bean (SHB) is found in Nicaragua.

TABLE 16: SHARE OF COFFEE CLASSIFIED AS HARD BEAN (HB) AND STRICTLY HARD BEAN (SHB)			
Country	**SHB (%)**	**HB (%)**	**SHB plus HB (%)**
Costa Rica	39	24	63
Guatemala	45	19	64
El Salvador	15	32	47
Nicaragua	85	N.A.	85 +
Honduras	19	67	86

Source: Estimates using data from the IDB country reports.

Obstacles to Improved Competitiveness

If Nicaragua has the necessary agro-ecological conditions to produce high quality coffee, what is stopping the country from taking more advantage of opportunities arising from consumer preferences for better quality and specialty coffees? In large part, much Nicaraguan coffee production suffers from inadequate production practices and post-harvest practices, and therefore lacks consistent quality. The country's producers also lack sufficient marketing and promotion of their products. In particular, Nicaraguan coffee production is characterized by:

- Inconsistent quality: inadequate regulatory framework and processes to preserve, standardize and guarantee the quality of Nicaraguan coffee.
- Insufficient marketing: lack of strategic plan for marketing and promoting the branding and quality of Nicaraguan coffee, particularly specialty coffee, internationally.
- High production costs as a result of low technological investments.
- Obsolete and inadequate processing infrastructure (wet and dry milling).
- Inadequate logistical infrastructure, such as storage facilities, ports, roads, etc.
- Poor knowledge and access to market instruments for hedging prices and managing risk.
- High levels of indebtedness of the medium and large producers that participated in the Renovation Program for Coffee Areas (1993–97).

Deterioration of coffee plantations due to neglect and abandonment by some 28,000 small producers due to lack of access to adequate financing.

Strategies to Improve Competitiveness

Quality control and improvement. Results from the "Cup of Excellence" competition held in Nicaragua in 2002 indicated there is significant potential for improving the quality of Nicaraguan coffee. Furthermore, a competition held under the auspices of the Specialty Coffee Association of America (SCAA) resulted in many finalists from Nicaragua. Continued work on improving quality control will be key for Nicaraguan coffee overall, but particularly for specialty coffees (organic, environmentally friendly, gourmet, etc.). Adoption of appropriate grading/quality standards (though regulations), improving processing (wet and dry milling) and reducing the quantity of coffee coming from sub-optimal areas (low altitudes) should be very important. Another effective approach may be to develop a quality map by zones of origin, which is a way to link regional quality control and improvement with a marketing campaign, as in an *appellation* system.

An approach suggested by officials of Nicaragua's Ministry of Agriculture and Forestry is to provide funding for those producers in low areas (below 800 meters), with low potential for producing quality coffee, to convert their coffee plantations into forests. Such a program would help producers in need, and would also contribute to raising the general quality level of Nicaraguan coffee.

An IDB/WB/USAID discussion document (2002) recommends quality improvement through improved education of farmers and establishment of local cupping laboratories in producing regions. Physical evaluation and cupping are procedures performed by coffee importers on samples they receive before shipment. The capacity for farmers to evaluate coffee with the same standards as buyers is key to generating better quality. Also, assuring commercial consistency in lots and confidence in delivery are essential to developing long-term relationships with buyers.

Quality control/improvement measures may include:

- Adequate preparation of coffee before and during harvest. This involves appropriate cultural and harvesting practices to ensure quality.
- Incentives for producing quality coffee in terms of a compensation system that recognizes and reward quality differences and effectively transmits price signals to producers.
- Improvements in transportation so deter quality deterioration during transport of cherries to the wet mills or coffee coming from wet mills.
- Support of producer organizations in developing organizational and cooperative approaches that will help improve managerial problems and improve quality. For example producer organization can disseminate quality standards and best practices in coffee farm care and harvest.

▓ Support the production of differentiated coffees by supporting necessary extension, training and certification of these coffees.

▓ Investments in appropriate equipment and practices to protect and enhance coffee quality.

▓ Cupping laboratories and training sessions established at the coffee mills to better evaluate the quality.

▓ Strengthening business and marketing practices at the mills so they better promote quality coffee and transmit rewards to farmers who deliver better quality.

Marketing, promotion and working with retailers. The "Cup of Excellence" competition held in Nicaragua in May, 2002, has contributed to creating a positive reputation for Nicaragua in the world coffee market. Activities to promote branding (labeling) and recognition of Nicaraguan coffee in specialty coffee markets, including gourmet, organic, environmentally friendly, etc., and would include participation in international and national events, such as the "Cup of Excellence" competition.

Another key approach can be to work directly with retailers. Indeed, retailers' ability to develop private labels and otherwise bypass the traditional trading channels is fast emerging as a critical competitive factor. Such labels are taking a fast-increasing share of grocery sales, even at the high-end of the market. Moreover, they do not require costly market entries or direct competition with current buyers. But there are demanding requirements in terms of quality, packaging, and "just in time" fulfillment that could be a difficult hurdle. Thus, only the more organized producer groups and associations will have the capacity to deal with retailers directly. Efforts to reduce dependence on middlemen could involve combining the resources of more than one organization into a second-tier or apex group that can then hire the person(s) with the appropriate skills, dedication, and time available to conduct those functions as a formal business.

Brand recognition is a valuable asset in an increasingly competitive coffee market. Colombia's achievement in this area took 50 years and a multimillion-dollar promotional budget, but several smaller Central American brands have also achieved a measure of market recognition and success. Brand development requires long-term investment and a strong commitment from all stakeholders involved in developing them. For producers that feature coffees with Geographic Indications of Origin, this means a coordinated quality commitment throughout the appellation that is necessarily born of a strong organizational structure. That structure is vital in order to provide adequate information and technical training to the farmers in that circumscribed area and to monitor compliance with the quality requirements of the appellation or brand. Government needs to support the mapping and development of adequate geographic indicators and must also enforce the regulations protecting them.

Investment in technology to cut production costs. Nicaragua could reduce production costs on average by an estimated US$10/quintal (QQ) through adoption of better technology. Yields could increase from current levels at 12 QQ/mz to 18 QQ/mz. To achieve this, the country needs to determine priorities for investing in appropriate technologies, including adopting organic and low-input production, rehabilitation of existing plantations, and crop diversification particularly in sub-optimal producing areas. Technical assistance and extension will play an important role in this.

Improvement in risk management. The coffee sector would largely benefit from improved education and training of farmers and other participants along the coffee commercialization chain in the use of risk management instruments. Making larger use of price risk management instruments will allow farmers to lock-in a minimum price for their crop and facilitate in obtaining credit since price insurance can insure the ability for repaying credit. Price risk management will allow banks and other financial institutions to offer loans that can have repayment provisions linked to world coffee prices. Although price risk management is by and large a private sector activity, the government could promote awareness and information perhaps through an office at the Ministry of Agriculture dedicated to technical assistance in risk management. Although it may be tempting to set-up a stabilization fund to support low prices, the international experience regarding stabilization funds has been dismal. Thus, it is strongly suggested that the government does not adopt such a strategy.

One way coffee producers can get access to risk management markets is through aggregating demand for risk management instruments, via producer organizations, cooperatives, rural credit institutions and traders. Some approaches include: *linking price insurance to a loan agreement; adopting sales management techniques,* such as hedging strategies, for cooperatives that manage sales on behalf of their members; *using inventory management; aggregating quantities for hedging;* and *using guarantee contracts* between farmer organizations and users (as with Fair Trade).

Incentive and strategic alliance. Nicaragua should take advantage of opportunities to add value to its coffee exports taking advantage of zero level import tariffs in the US and European Union. Higher value added in exports of coffee products could be achieved through: appropriate incentives such as tax heavens for companies willing to invest in processing of raw materials locally; and by encouraging the formation of strategic alliances with international companies involved in the distribution and food processing in major consuming countries.

Organizational development. The quality and capacity of local organizations and associations is a critical factor in the success of any quality-control, technology-enhancement or marketing project. Unfortunately, most producer organizations are inadequately assessed for their capacity to participate effectively. As a result, projects are stalled, monitoring costs skyrocket, and shortcuts are eventually cobbled together in order to get by and proceed. There are probably only a handful of Central American cooperatives that require no institutional support and training in order to be effective partners. Therefore, projects may need to incorporate institutional support in the form of: improving management capacity; initiating or strengthening internal accounting systems; strengthening democratic processes through representativeness, information flow and formal legitimacy.

Defining public vs. private roles - seeking private-sector "match-makers". For either improving competitiveness in coffee or diversifying out of coffee, the public sector can have an important role in providing public goods such as information (for example, research and extension) and infrastructure. The private sector, both domestic and foreign, should take the lead in identifying opportunities and facilitating the adoption of appropriate technologies and arranging for financial and marketing arrangements. What might be needed are *match makers* (that is, firms with knowledge of local conditions and links with domestic and foreign entrepreneurs) who can identify opportunities and help match private sector firms with producers and producer groups.

3

IMPROVING FACTOR MARKETS

W hile promoting the competitiveness of Nicaraguan agriculture should be at the heart of immediate policy measures to be undertaken by the current administration, these immediate measures will also have to be complemented by sustained, ongoing efforts, initiated over the past decade and still in progress, to improve factor market efficiency. This chapter briefly reviews four factor markets that bear directly on agricultural investment and productivity—rural finance, agricultural technology, land and rural labor—and recommends measures to improve them.

Rural Finance

Credit flows from Nicaraguan banks to the domestic private sector as a whole increased between 1995 and 2001 by 330 percent in real terms, climbing from 34 to 104 percent of GDP. However, loan disbursements to the agriculture sector, in contrast, declined by 2.4 percent over the same period. Credit to agriculture as a share of agricultural GDP initially had risen from 20 to 43 percent between 1995 and 1999 (prior to the sharp decline in coffee prices), but then fell back to 14 percent of GDP by the end of 2001. This decline in lending to agriculture, both in terms of real volume and as a share of agricultural production, took place even while agricultural output continued to rise steadily.

That agricultural credit flows from banks were cut in half over the last two years, while production rose by 16 percent, indicates that producers generally were likely to rely more on equity, retained earnings, savings and commercial credit suppliers[17] in order to finance operations. While real interest rates on Cordoba-denominated loans declined between 1995 and 2000, annual rates on dollar-denominated loans, which constitute more than 85 percent of bank portfolios, increased by one percentage point to a rate of about 17 percent (Rodríguez and Saveedra 2000). Commercial

---

17. "Commercial credit suppliers" here refers not to banks but rather to traders of agricultural inputs who extend credit to farmers.

33

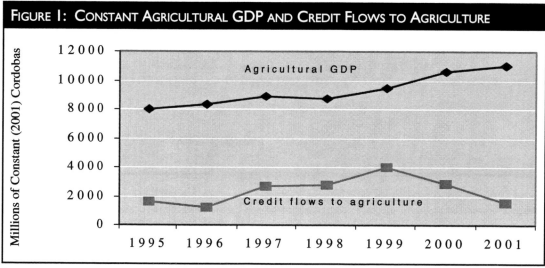

FIGURE 1: CONSTANT AGRICULTURAL GDP AND CREDIT FLOWS TO AGRICULTURE

Source: BCN 2002.

credit suppliers, which were providing lending to agriculture at levels nearly equal to banks in 1997 (the last year for which the Central Bank collected data on these suppliers), generally charge higher rates of interest than banks (Robinson 2001).

In rural areas, one-fifth of rural households obtained credit from any source in 1998, and commercial credit suppliers were by far the most common source of finance (Sánchez 2001). Access to institutional lenders was rare in rural areas; only 2 percent of households received loans from banks, 2.9 percent from microfinance NGOs, and 1.4 percent borrowed from mutual savings and loan associations, such as cooperatives and credit unions; only 3 percent of rural households held financial savings in 1998 (Sánchez 2001).

That the availability of financial services is limited and the cost of credit high in rural areas has serious implications for economic growth and welfare in Nicaragua. Households derive considerable economic benefits from access to safe and interest-bearing savings instruments, both through the direct income effects of earning positive returns on liquid assets and the ability to self-insure against

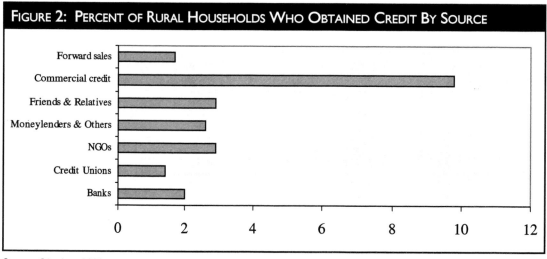

FIGURE 2: PERCENT OF RURAL HOUSEHOLDS WHO OBTAINED CREDIT BY SOURCE

Source: Sánchez 2000.

shocks, for instance. The terms and availability of credit directly affects household welfare in the short and medium terms and, on a broad scale, the volume of credit flows relative to GDP influence economic growth over time. Scarce and costly loans may also negatively affect investment in agriculture relatively more than others sectors, as agriculture has been shown to be relatively more capital intensive than non-agriculture in a large sample of developing countries (Mundlak 1997, cited in Schiff and Váldes 1998).

Key Issues and Bottlenecks

Improving the terms and access to financial services in rural areas requires increased efficiency and competition among an array of providers, including banks, finance companies, savings and credit cooperatives, input suppliers, equipment dealers, and warehouses, for example. This requires a consistent and appropriate regulatory framework for providers of like financial services, basic financial sector infrastructure, and a consistent approach for targeting donor and government support to financial services industry development based on achieving unsubsidized private sector competition.

Private commercial banks and finance companies play an extremely important role in the industry and in the economy as providers of finance and savings instruments and as nodes in the payment services system. While banks have cut loans to agriculture over the last several years due in part to the fall in coffee prices, at end-year 2001 the portfolio of bank loans in the sector (US$284 million) was still more than six times the total combined portfolio of the 13 largest microfinance NGOs (US$39.5 million) and the 18 largest credit unions (US$4.4 million) (Vickers and Baumgardt 2002). The number of bank branches outside of Managua has approximately doubled since 1995 and, system-wide, savings deposits have increased by 80 percent in real terms. A sample of rural bank branches analyzed recently shows, however, that banks originate very few loans at these facilities. (World Bank 2001f). For Nicaragua's formal financial institutions to respond on a large scale to the changing terms of trade and incentive structures shaping productive opportunities in rural areas, they must have regulations and infrastructure which facilitate increased outreach to new clients engaged in different economic activities.

The high costs and risks involved in lending to unknown rural clients, particularly on a smaller-scale, are among the reasons formal financial institutions have not exploited these markets. Deficiencies in financial systems infrastructure contribute to theses costs and risks rather than helping to mitigate them. An inefficient and little-used system for evaluating borrower creditworthiness, for instance, adds substantially to the costs and risks of lending to borrowers who have little other than their "reputational" collateral. Asymmetric information problems surrounding borrowers' intentions and capacity to repay loans tend to translate into higher prices and a smaller supply of lending, just as economic theory predicts, and these problems tend to be most pronounced in the small business segment of the market (Galindo and Miller 2001). Recent evidence suggests that efficiently collecting, distributing and analyzing borrowers' historical financial information in a standardized fashion substantially reduces the risks and transaction costs of credit delivery. In Nicaragua, payment histories are scarcely used to gain credit or shop for better terms among lenders due to limited reporting of information. Problems in the legal and institutional framework for securing loans with physical collateral also constrain financial flows in rural areas due to the costliness and uncertainty involved in registering asset pledges, determining creditor priority and repossessing collateral. The supply of credit to rural areas may be especially limited by the inability of equipment dealers, input suppliers and producers to leverage their stocks of accounts receivables, inventories and crops, for example, to secure additional credit.

Legal norms and regulatory standards may discourage banks and finance companies from pursuing new borrowers in rural areas, especially smaller-scale clients. Regulatory barriers to entry into the small scale and rural markets, such as the standards and methods used to evaluate borrower repayment capacity and guarantee quality for microloan classification and provisioning requirements, for example, may inhibit banks and finance companies from pursuing new clients in these niches. Among the households who obtained credit in 1998, the median loan amount was US$136 (Sánchez 2001); this figure underscores the importance of effectively encouraging banks and finance companies to effectively manage the particular costs and risks associated with micro loan portfolios if they are going to serve a significant portion of the credit consuming households in Nicaragua. Norms applied to loan processing, product mixes, and branch hours and facilities may also impose limitations on institutions pursing new instruments and methods for reaching new clientele, particularly in rural areas.

Government and donor financed credit programs and institutions distort credit markets and have detrimental effects on the welfare of poor households. Donor and government support to small-scale and rural financial markets is generally concentrated in providing subsidized lines of credit for selected activities and populations, and directly supporting microfinance institutions. Subsidized lines of credit are administered by banks, finance companies, NGOs, and cooperatives on the retail level, as channelled to them directly by donors, or primarily through three public institutions: the Nicaraguan Investment Fund (Financiera Nicaragüense de Inversión—FNI), the Rural Credit Fund (Fondo de Crédito Rural—FCR), and the Rural Development Institute (Instituto de Desarrollo Rural—IDR). Recent estimates of the rural portfolios of the three latter institutions combined amount to about US$79 million, only a fraction of which is considered recoverable.[18] Consultations with banks indicate that they are currently administering about US$40 million in targeted credit programs funded by donors, and numerous other programs are administered by NGOs, cooperatives and finance companies. These interventions are likely to have distorting effects upon credit markets by creating disincentives for finance companies and banks to pursue donor program beneficiaries with commercially priced credit. Credit programs with significant transfer components tend to be very poor and costly safety net mechanisms.

High cost loans have detrimental welfare effects upon poor borrowers. Donor and government support to targeted sectors of the economy and to microfinance NGOs and which establish increased access to credit as an objective of their interventions may actually be contributing to the poverty of borrowers rather than helping to alleviate it. Legovini (2002) analyzes the short and medium-term impact of cash borrowing on household welfare and business performance in Nicaragua using panel data, and concludes that the effects upon the poor are strongly negative: "Simulations on poverty indicators show that when the availability of cash loans expands, poverty incidence, depth and severity may increase."

Encouraging sustainability-oriented microfinance NGOs to work towards conversion into formal, commercial finance companies is vital for stimulating fair competition among providers of financial services and achieving lower effective interest rates for borrowers. The number of branches of microfinance NGOs in Nicaragua is roughly equivalent to the number of bank branches; these institutions serve more than 100,000 clients and have received tens of millions of dollars of donor support in recent years (Vickers and Baumgardt 2002).[19] Despite high levels of support to microfinance NGOs resulting in an average cost of funds recently estimated to be around -7.9 percent in real terms, the effective interest rates NGOs charge borrowers reportedly average more than 75 percent per year, though ranging widely among institutions and programs (Sánchez 2001). Subsidies are targeted to microfinance NGOs absent any uniform auditing, accounting or performance standards, or consistent goals, in terms of the ultimate position of these institutions in the formal financial sector. Considerable progress has been made in the development of commercially viable microlenders—two NGOs have recently converted or applied for licenses to operate as finance companies, and a recent study shows that three others have attained financial self-sufficiency (Nusselder and Sanders 2002). However, donors and NGOs on the whole have yet to adopt conversion into finance companies as generally an achievable and desirable objective for serious microfinance institutions. Experience indicates that "large-scale microfinance,

---

18. These estimates are based on recent discussions with government officials.

19. Recent consultations indicate that programs in support of microfinance NGOs currently under implementation amount to more than US$20 million as funded by four donors alone (Vickers and Baumgardt 2002).

sustainable over time, can be attained only in financially self-sufficient commercial institutions in the formal financial sector." (Robinson 2001). Competition on a level regulatory playing field is also the most effective way to encourage increased efficiency among financial service providers and lower the costs of their services.

Cooperative savings and credit institutions have the potential to reach greater numbers of rural communities with basic savings and credit services, but absent proper safeguards, may present considerable risks to poorer depositors. The framework for the regulation and development of credit unions and cooperatives in Nicaragua provides inadequately for the regulation and supervision larger deposit mobilizing institutions, which currently manage approximately US$1.7 million savings deposits. Meanwhile the potential for small, closed cooperatives to provide basic savings and credit services in more isolated rural communities has yet to be developed.

Recommended Areas for Action
Government, in consultation with the private sector, and in coordination with the donor community, should take the lead in addressing the key issues outlined above, giving priority to:

- Developing a strategy of support for expanding access and lowing the cost of financial services not through subsidized credit or institutionalized support to intermediaries, but rather through regulations that encourage fair competition among providers of like services, the provision of basic financial systems infrastructure, and the creation of technically knowledgeable public institutions that can play effective oversight roles.
- Identifying and revising overly restrictive, costly or inappropriate regulations and enforcement standards (in terms of microloan risk classification and provisioning requirements, evaluation of borrower repayment capacity, or new product development, for instance) that inhibit banks and finance companies from safely pursuing new market segments, including smaller and rural households and businesses.
- Targeting limited donor and government funds for financial institution development by using incentives and standardized performance measures to encourage microfinance NGOs' progress along a path towards commercial viability and formal sector membership.
- Establishing a regulatory and development framework that provides mutual savings and credit associations with a sound institutional development path and framework for protecting client savings.
- Establishing the legal framework and operational infrastructure needed to more efficiently and reliably manage credit risks through credit information and collateral pledging systems.
- Conducting a thorough assessment of regulations and institutions to determine key barriers to the growth and development of an integrated financial system and sound private sector development framework in rural areas. Examples of subjects worth evaluating include bankruptcy laws and business registration procedures, auditing and accounting standards, insurance and capital markets, and mortgage and storage finance, for instance.

Agricultural Technology
Agricultural growth during the last six years averaged 9 percent annually. However, increased agricultural production has mainly been the result of an expansion in the land area under cultivation, largely for basic grains and in marginal lands, rather than increases in productivity through improved technology and innovation. The continuous use of under-productive marginal land poses clear and definite limits to the sustainable expansion of agricultural production. Productivity increases will depend therefore on pushing outwards the production frontier rather then the agricultural frontier, on increasing the efficiency of input use, and on sustaining the resource base.

Agricultural research and technical assistance have constituted, during the last few years, important policy instruments of the Nicaraguan Government in support of small- and medium-scale farm households. In 1993, with assistance from the World Bank, the Government articulated a comprehensive strategy for the agricultural sector incorporated in the design of the Agricultural Technology and Land Management Project, (ATLMP) leading to the creation of the Nicaraguan Institute of Agricultural Technology (INTA). In 2001 the government launched a longer-term investment in an agricultural technology program that integrates public and private research, technical assistance and education & training as a cohesive, integrated agricultural knowledge based system. Within this strategy, the establishment of the Nicaraguan Foundation for Agricultural Technology (Fundación Nicaragüense de Tecnología Agropecuaria - FUNICA) sent a strong signal of the government's intention to follow through in establishing an effective public-private partnership. While INTA would strengthen its role as a public service provider, FUNICA would administer a competitive fund with lines for research, extension, and eventually other services: the Agricultural Research Competitive Fund (Fondo de Apoyo a la Investigación Tecnológica Agropecuaria de Nicaragua - FAITAN) is up-scaling INTA's pilot experience since 1993, and the Fund for Technical Assistance (Fondo de Asistencia Técnica - FAT) is being tested in León and Chinandega.

Key Issues and Bottlenecks

Agricultural research and extension will be more important in increasing productivity in the future than it has been in the past but, by themselves, they will be insufficient elements to promote innovation and technological changes. In contrast, these could be achieved by gradually integrating farmers, educators, researchers and extension agents within one system of knowledge and information. While government has been proactively pursuing the creation of a broader, integrated system (SINTA), the following issues still need to be addressed.

Low coverage of extension services. Even though during the nineties INTA, other government's initiatives (IDR), and NGO's have succeeded in increasing farmer's access to advisory services, their overall utilization remains low. Only 15 percent of farm households make use of advisory services, and only half of them are provided by the Government.

Incoherent research agenda. Many different activities funded by the government and donors are pushing the technological agenda in different directions without a shared strategic vision. It is not really a matter of resources, but an issue of utilization and impact.

Shallow penetration of the information available. The country lacks an effective technological information system that maps and evaluate channels for agricultural knowledge flows, and that integrates existing useful knowledge to meet the demand of information of farmers, extension agents, researchers and government agencies.

Disconnect between public and private sector. Scientists conducting agricultural research, providing extension and training services in National Agrarian University (Universidad Nacional Agraria (UNA), Central American University (Universidad Centro Americana (UCA), Universidad Nacional de Nicaragua (UNAN), INTA, National Institute of Technology (INATEC) and development NGO's, to a large extent are working in isolation with no effective linkages among them, with competing resources, and no clear impact in their activities.

Low technical education. High levels of illiteracy in poor farm households (32 percent in agricultural areas and 40 percent amongst the poorest), and limited schooling among young people (62 percent of 15–39 year-olds have only 3 years) have recently been recognized as a leading cause for the delayed rate of implementation of innovative agricultural technologies, thwarted diversification of the agricultural economy, and perpetuated agricultural/urban divide.

Recommended Areas for Action

Developing an agricultural knowledge and information system and making it responsive to farmers' needs will require:

▓ Repositioning INTA: In a free market environment where advisory services can effectively be offered by a number of actors, the public sector should concentrate on creating a policy and regulatory environment and on improving the quality of services that only the government can offer. The Nicaraguan Institute for Agricultural Technology's (INTA's) new role as a second-tier institution should, among other functions: (i) focus *public-good* related research and maintain strategic research programs of national interest, (ii) serve as the "think-tank" in agricultural technology issues, including biotechnology, (iii) become the technology bank for the agricultural sector and diffuse those technologies to service providers, (iv) open up the regional research centers to local stakeholders in setting up the research agenda, and (v) maintain strong linkages with international institutions and networks associated with the Consultative Group on International Agricultural Research (CGIAR, such as CIMMYT, CIAT, etc.), and adapt the developed genetic materials to local conditions.

- Supporting FUNICA: FUNICA's role in the medium term should be at the center of MAG-FOR attention by making it a functional forum for consensus building among public and private actors represented therein. Through FUNICA, Government could launch competitive calls and awarding research activities among different research institutions, establish partnerships with overseas universities of high reputation, and develop a competitive fund for extension and eventually other activities (technical education, marketing, pre-investments, etc.).

- Developing a competitive market for agricultural training: The success of technology transfer and adoption depends *inter alia* upon regular training of technical assistance providers as well as receivers; The communication between researchers, extension agents and farmers can be facilitated by (i) "training the trainers" programs aiming at updating scientific knowledge and skills of service providers; (ii) a reform of the system of agricultural technical education, so as to open up and to provide opportunities to private service providers. Strengthening the institutional capacity of INATEC to manage this process will demonstrate to be key to the success of this initiative; (iii) the strengthening of human resources for the public agricultural sector with regular training to key technical staff of MAGFOR, INTA, INATEC, IDR and INAFOR.

- Increasing the flow of information: As markets are playing a more important role in the decision-making process of producers, the importance of an integrated market and price information system could have a large payoff. This could be achieved by integrating different existing subsystems related to agricultural prices, marketing, technology and training, with links to regional and international data bases (CGIAR, IICA, FAO, etc.).

Land Access and Tenure Insecurity

Nicaragua has inherited a highly inequitable structure of land ownership. A land reform under which the Government distributed large amounts of land without providing clear legal title to it has given rise to a wave of restitution claims that have, both administratively and financially, constituted a huge burden for every Government since the early 1990s. The distribution of land ownership remains highly inequitable, with a Gini coefficient of 0.86. Coupled with this, weak institutional and legal frameworks and years of legal and administrative decisions affecting land rights have contributed to hindering the fair and definitive recognition and adjudication of land rights, provoking profound and lasting land-tenure insecurity (particularly in but not restricted to the rural areas). The magnitude of this problem is enormous, both in terms of fiscal spending and in terms of the resulting tenure insecurity.

Tenure insecurity is not only related to the lack of formal ownership documentation (title or deed) or to the lack of registration. It is also strongly linked to the flood of claims for restitution of the confiscated or expropriated land after 1979, which continues nowadays, in spite of various efforts aimed at setting an end to the lodging of new claims by former owners. This has made the rights of agrarian reform beneficiaries contingent upon a case-by-case review of these claims.

One of the main problems that the sector faces is the institutional incapability to adequately complete the allocations. Currently, a significant number of ex-combatants are in possession of properties (once administered by CORNAP) whose land rights and purchase-sale contracts have not been completed either because they were assigned by means of a provisional allocation by INRA (now OTR) in a rapid fashion, subject to going through a formal land-titling process, or because the purchase the government had to make as a result of land invasions by armed groups were not registered previously to the transfer to the new owners. In fact, in a number of cases the state increased the insecurity due to the lack of veridical information or the precarious solutions permitted (such as, *Titulos Supletorios)*.

Key Issues and Bottlenecks

Legal framework is inappropriate. In general terms, the legal framework governing the "land reform sector" is not appropriate to handle issues of land tenure security in a systematic and non-regressive manner. The complexity of its operational regulations impede the speeding up of the resolution of thousands of pending cases that await administrative action prior to the definitive recognition of rights. The centralized and multiplicity of state entities dealing with land rights and related legal services, coupled with the fact that the legislation is almost silent with respect to the non-reform sector, definitely aggravates the already an inadequate legal framework.

Institutional reforms are not completed. Institutionally, the agrarian sector has been a victim of erratic reforms and policies. More than twelve different institutions have legal authority to define (or deny) land rights and several entities were specially created to enforce specific land-related laws or decrees (for example, OCI, OOT, CNRC, etc.). Even though some of these institutions are now grouped under the Intendencia de la Propiedad, this institution lacks the necessary hierarchy, clear mandate and resources to deal with the various land tenure regimes and their current complexity.

Lack of confidence in the regulatory framework. Socially, the intention had been to use land as a means for creating social unity and for rebuilding peace: First, by the Sandinistas in an attempt to redress the most flagrant inequities; Second, by the democratic process in an attempt to compensate ex-combatants and consolidate the disarmed process. In both cases, success has been mixed, and land remains today a potential source for major conflict and violence. In fact, the uncertainty prevailing in the countryside is quite high, with frequent open conflicts and land invasions. This general lack of confidence in the regulatory framework and the state institutions responsible for the administration of land rights represents a major challenge for the design of remedial measures.

Transaction costs remain high. Due to the centralized decision-making structure and the misconception of allocating land rights through demand-driven mechanisms, transaction costs for access to land and for land tenure security are extremely high, affecting mainly small and poor farmers.

Current landholding patterns are not maximizing productivity. Improperly documented property rights impede the efficient operations of land markets. Yet, those markets can be a powerful tool for redistributing land in an efficiency-enhancing way. Indeed, when land rights are easily transferred, whether through rentals or sales, from less efficient to more efficient producers, the effect will be to allocate land to its more productive use. At the same time, growing international evidence shows that family-based farms tend to make more efficient use of labor than wage-labor farms. Thus, well-functioning markets will tend to reallocate land to smaller farms, and thereby be both efficiency- and equity-enhancing.

Larger-scale producers use less labor and are less productive. The general case is supported by empirical evidence in Nicaragua. The country has a highly unequal land ownership distribution, and a negative relationship between agricultural profits and the size of area operated by a given producer. The mean profit per *manzana* for large producers is about ten times less than what is obtained by small producers. This is paralleled by large differences in labor intensity. Small livestock farms spend almost 40 times more labor than large ranches, and even on coffee farms and other types of operation, labor input in the group of large producers is more than 10 times less than what is used on small farms. This implies that well-functioning markets could equalize input intensities.

Land rental remains limited and therefore is not exerting its full potential to effect beneficial redistribution. In fact, aggregate measures such as the Gini coefficient show a slight reduction in inequality from 0.86 to 0.80 as one moves from owned to operational landholdings, indicating that the land rental market does exert a moderately equalizing effect. Some 23 percent of all producers rent land, mainly the landless (18 percent of producers) but also some landowners (5 percent of producers). Clearly, land rentals remain of limited scope. Their limited scope means they fail to massively redistribute land from large units (that are relatively less productive) to small units (that are relatively more productive), thereby foregoing an important opportunity to equalize land productivity, and improve land access by poor smallholders (Deininger 2001).

Land sales patterns are raising rather than lessening concentration of ownership. As for land sales, the trend is opposite that which one would expect from well-functioning markets. In the active land market of the last five years, with 2 percent of all producers buying, there has been no net transfer of land to small producers, despite the fact that a large number of them participated in the market. The amount of net purchases was in all types of operations greater for large farms than for small farms, effectively leading to re-concentration. It appears that most of the net accumulation has been concentrated with large coffee and livestock producers. Unavailability of credit, which constrains small-farmer demand, and distorted land prices caused by investment of non-agricultural assets, are likely to be the main market imperfections. Recent investigations have found that with regard to land access and its equity dimension, the attractiveness of speculative land accumulation is still significant although an incipient redistribution trend could be identified. The latter was based on rental markets shifting land from large to small producers (Deininger and Lavadenz 2001).

Formally documented and easily transferable land rights are lacking. The evidence suggests that lack of formally documented land rights and resulting insecurity of property rights has a distinct impact on land markets. This strengthens the case for a speedy and comprehensive resolution of Nicaragua's pervasive land tenure problem. Independently of the justification for such a measure in terms of economic efficiency, there is a strong justification in terms of equity. Additional measures would be useful to further stimulate rental markets, in order to reduce transaction costs associated with entering and enforcing rental contracts.

Recommended Areas for Action

The land tenure situation suggests the need to follow a dual strategy. On the one hand the implementation of a land rights regularization program and, on the other, targeted interventions towards improving land access. The latter can be achieved both through the functioning of land markets and through completion of the land redistribution process that is already underway in some areas. Such an approach will involve regulatory as well as institutional reforms and will amount to a profound revision of land policy revision. Within this approach, the following actions should be considered:

- Move from land titling towards a systematic process of regularization of property in rural as well as urban areas: Even though land tenure insecurity is pervasive throughout Nicaragua, there are certain areas where the problem is particularly severe and where the main problem appears to be lack of institutional capacity. Dealing with these areas (such as, cooperatives) in a speedy manner will allow success in dealing with the issues and, at the same time, help to establish approaches to address the broader legal and restitution issues. In addition, full registration has proved to be a significant need in Nicaragua. It implies that land rights registration have to be made accessible and affordable to beneficiaries.
- Eliminate land ownership insecurity by addressing constraints and reform priorities: Major constraints are related to the existing legal and regulatory framework which includes unclear and dispersed rules of the game; contradictory laws and regulations; limitations to ownership rights; demand-driven and case by case revisions, unreliable land titles (i.e. *titulos supletorios*) and inconsistencies in the overall land legislation. Reforms must include institutional re-engineering, decentralization land-related services provision, delegation to the local level

of a number of decision-making processes; simplifying procedures for land rights allocation and registration; unifying the legal framework, lifting its limitations on land ownership and ensuring its consistency with other sectors; establishing a modern land administration system; and reducing costs for the poor.

▨ Complete institutional reforms: The Government has started to move towards a more effective, accessible, and streamlined institutional structure for the administration of land rights. Further actions are needed before embarking in a large scale regularization/titling effort. These may comprise: (i) an autonomous Intendance of Property (rural and urban), with a higher rank in the hierarchy and a decentralized organization with strong departmental representation; (ii) an integrated cadastral and registration systems; (iii) a linkage between the integrated cadastral and registration systems and the municipalities, who would use the territorial information as a foundation for the fiscal cadastre and territorial planning; (iv) an autonomous Cadastre branch separate from INETER due to the multiplicity of other competences such as the geological and climatological services; (v) a modernized Public Registry of Property that include the use of modern technology and updated information to register and protect rights; (vi) the elimination of overlapping responsibilities (such as, between the Intendance and the *Procuraduría del Estado* in assigning land or between OTR and the civil judges in granting land titles); and (vii) alternative conflict resolution mechanisms for ensuring prompt and expedite dispute resolution before or during the land regularization process.

▨ Improve the functioning of land markets: The paradox of widespread underutilization of land and at the same time lack of land access needs to be resolved by utilizing markets as one means to provide better access to land. This would encompass promotion of longer-term land rental contracts, provision of information on land prices to potential participants, and elimination of remaining restrictions on such markets. Also, the pros and cons of a land tax should be considered.

▨ Address the special case of indigenous lands: It is crucial to define criteria and procedures for the titling and demarcation of indigenous peoples lands. Although the Constitution of Nicaragua recognizes communal land rights for indigenous communities in the Atlantic Coast, no law translates this principle into concrete norms and procedures that, at this time could allow for secure and incontestable titling of communal land. Importantly such a law would need to clarify the treatment of landholders within the indigenous lands, and the indigenous rights to natural resources. There exists currently two law proposals in the National Assembly: one prepared by the Government, the other prepared with broad indigenous community representation. These two laws need to be revisited, and a consensus built around a single proposal, through a broad based dialogue that involves all stakeholders (including affected landholders of the respective areas, and not only the State and indigenous people). The existing legal framework being insufficient for definitive titling, brought upon conflictive interpretations about the roles of the communities, the traditional land occupancy and access to natural resources.

Rural Labor Market

Nicaraguans are a highly mobile population and work force. In the past, migration was driven mostly by political reasons, nowadays the people of Nicaragua migrate primarily for economic reasons and display every conceivable pattern of migration.[20] Migration is facilitated by the flexibility shown by Nicaraguan families to accommodate widely varying numbers of family members residing under one roof at different times of the year. The high mobility of the Nicaraguan labor market makes it more responsive to changing needs.

---

20. This section is based on the main findings of Ureta (2002) and of Ilahi (2000).

Key Issues and Bottlenecks

While on balance the labor market in Nicaragua works well, analysis of the most recent LSMS data shows that a number of issues stand out.

The demand for labor in the agricultural sector has dropped at a brisk pace in the past few years. The reasons for the decline are varied. Cotton used to be an important agricultural activity in Nicaragua, but the production of cotton is now virtually nonexistent. For decades coffee was the backbone of the agricultural sector. In the past four years, as production levels in Vietnam reached record levels, the price of coffee in the international market declined steadily and is now about a third of the peak reached in the decade of the 1990s. The beef/dairy industry has yet to recover from the war years when the herds were decimated. The sugar industry has also declined in recent years. Some of the sugar mills (*ingenios*) have closed and only five remain in operation.

These recent developments are reflected in the composition of employment in agriculture. The table below presents the distribution of agricultural sector workers across sub-categories (3-digit industry categories) of the agricultural sector. The category of basic grains, cereals, and other crops, which includes sugar cane, account for 60 percent of employment. Mixed exploitation, that is, animal husbandry in addition to other agricultural products is a distant second, accounting for only 15 percent of total employment. Category number 113 accounts for a mere 7 percent of employment, a controversial number that could be explained by the recent coffee crisis.

TABLE 17: SHARE OF AGRICULTURAL SECTOR WORKERS IN EACH 3-DIGIT INDUSTRY CATEGORY	
Three-digit industry categories	**Percent**
111 Basic grains, cereals, and other crops	59.9
112 Produce, legumes, and greenhouse products	3.3
113 Fruits, nuts, and plants whose leaves or fruits are used in the manufacture of beverages	7.2
121 Husbandry of cattle, sheep, goats, horses, donkeys, mules, etc.	10.5
122 Husbandry of other animals, and manufacture of animal products	0.8
130 Mixed exploitation: agricultural products together with animal husbandry	14.9
140 Farming and ranching services, excluding veterinary services	0.4
150 Hunting	0.0
200 Forestry	1.0
500 Fishing	1.7
No response	0.2
Total	100.0

Source: 2001 Mecovi Survey.

Lack of education and child labor constrain skilled labor supply. Although literacy campaigns during the 1980s expanded the number of people with basic reading and writing skills, formal schooling was disrupted to the point where the cohorts of youngsters who would have attended school during the war years have the lowest levels of formal completed schooling of similar aged cohorts in Latin America. Formal schooling of those cohorts is particularly acute for rural residents. Furthermore, the incidence of child labor in Nicaragua is about 11 percent and it is especially high in rural areas.[21] Many more boys work (17 percent) than girls (5 percent). In rural areas, almost 27 percent of all boys work and child labor tends to be high in farm households. Working children pay heavy penalties in terms of educational achievement as they spend roughly 31 hours per

---

21. The 1998 LSMS in World Band (2001c) defines child labor as the proportion of those in the 10-14 age group who work.

week in labor activities. Compared to being only at school, combining school and work slows educational attainment. Grade-for-age of those children who are in school-only is 65 percent versus 21 percent for those who only work.

Labor productivity and hence wages in the agricultural sector are notoriously low. Economic reform and restructuring in the mid-1990s have altered the structure of employment in Nicaragua. High-paying sectors such as construction, transport and financial services now have a higher but still small share of employment, starting from a very low base, but with wages increasing in real terms. For manufacturing, the share of employment and the level of wages have declined substantially, suggesting that this sector of activity has not picked up. Labor productivity on average in Nicaragua declined in the early 1990s with the agricultural sector recording the lowest productivity compared to other sectors in the economy. Younger generations have very low levels of formal schooling and cannot profit from access to improved methods of cultivation. The combined effect of these factors is that labor productivity and hence wages in the agricultural sector are notoriously low. All in all, labor productivity in the sector is on an upswing but is still the second-lowest in Central America, just above Honduras.[22]

In sum, in the agricultural sector there is scant capital with which to work, and the younger generation lacks the skill necessary to work the land. They didn't learn traditional methods of cultivation from their parents and their very low levels of formal schooling mean they cannot profit from access to improved seeds or methods of cultivation: they cannot read and follow instructions. The combined effect of these factors is that labor productivity and hence wages in the agricultural sector are notoriously low.

Incentives present in Nicaragua today discourage participation in the formal sector of the economy. This is especially true in rural areas. Wages in the agricultural sector are the lowest of all sectors of the economy, and display the most compressed distribution. The table below shows where the legally set minimum wage is located relative to the actual wages received by workers. The first two columns show, for each industry grouping, the minimum wage level established in March 2001. The next six columns are arranged in three pairs, for each of three categories of workers: "Employees" (permanent employees), "All Workers" (including employees plus temporary or seasonal workers) and "All Rural Resident Workers" (same as the "All Workers" category but including only workers who reside in rural areas). For each category of employee, a first column shows the actual, average monthly earnings received, and a second column indicates which centile, of the given employee group, is earning at the minimum wage level. Thus, for example, in agriculture, the minimum wage is located at the 26th centile of the distribution of "Employees," meaning that 26 percent of all permanent employees working in the agricultural sector are currently earning monthly wages below the legal minimum wage.

The figures show that the minimum wage for agriculture is at a relatively high centile along the distribution of actual earnings, compared with other industries; that is, a relatively high percentage of agricultural workers are receiving actual earnings below the legally set minimum wage level. For example, in the "All Workers" category, a full 39 percent of workers earn less than the minimum wage in agriculture, second only to construction. This suggests that the effects of the current minimum wage on employment might be worth examining: it is possible that a lower minimum wage would allow producers to employ more labor in the formal sector. If the minimum wage is not enforced whatsoever, of course, then it is probably having little effect. But there exists some consensus that, by and large, businesses operating in the formal sector of the economy do abide by minimum wage laws; that is, the medium- and large-scale agricultural producers do pay the minimum wage.

Empirical evidence produced for this report (see volume II) suggests that the level of the minimum wage is set sufficiently high along the overall distribution of earnings to be binding in the

---

22. The recent increase in productivity in the agricultural sector may be due, in part, a result of the coffee export boom experienced in Nicaragua during that period.

Industry	Minimum wage (monthly earnings)	Permanent Employees		All Workers		All Rural Workers	
		Average monthly earnings	% earning less than minimum wage	Average monthly earnings	% earning less than minimum wage	Average monthly earnings	% earning less than minimum wage
Agriculture	550	966	26	1037	39	947	40
Fishing & Services	785	1765	26	2061	32	11738	35
Mining	950	1418	36	1488	37	1695	30
Manufacture	670	1773	13	1690	21	1541	3
Water, power, commerce, transp.	1010	2169	27	2693	35	1708	43
Construction	1300	2048	52	2081	48	1820	56
Financial institutions & insurance	1120	6018	8	5392	10	1716	14
Government	630	3444	3	3444	3	2333	7

TABLE 18: MINIMUM WAGES RELATIVE TO AVERAGE WAGES IN 2001, BY INDUSTRY (Córdobas)

Source: 2001 Mecovi Survey.

formal sector of the economy. For the agricultural sector, the current level is 580 Córdobas or about US$41.1 per month.

There is a proposal to modify existing law in order to index minimum wages to the prevailing exchange rate. Such a measure may exert downward pressure on formal-sector employment. If the current minimum wage level is in fact an obstacle to the creation of more formal-sector jobs, as suggested by the background paper on this subject in volume II, this problem could be exacerbated by any legislation requiring that the structure of minimum wages be automatically revised to maintain US dollar-denominated purchasing power. Such a measure amounts to adding downward wage inflexibility (relative to the dollar), an effect that policy makers may want to avoid in the interest of encouraging more formal sector employment.

Recommended Areas for Action

Conditional on the institutional and policy framework present in the Nicaraguan economy today, the labor market functions well. However, rural sector wages are considerably lower than they can be, the demand for labor is depressed, the work force lacks basic skills, and payroll taxes are too high. The following areas for action should be therefore be considered as priority:

- Growth in the demand for labor in rural sectors requires that producers have access to reasonably priced credit. In turn, this requires that landowners be given clear title to their land. If Nicaragua is to achieve export-led growth, products have to be shipped to market at competitive cost and speed. Increases in human capital are essential for growth in labor productivity and wages. To encourage school attendance and learning by rural children, the children have to be fed while at school. The children should be given uniforms, and families should be spared the tuition cost and cost of school materials. As for young adults, the myriad of internationally and nationally funded technical training programs has to be coordinated and given focus. A promising approach is to link technical training efforts to the current work aimed at developing clusters of competitiveness.
- Perhaps the greatest obstacle to the accumulation of human capital by low-skilled workers who are no longer of school age is the present structure of minimum wages. First, high

minimum wages greatly discourage the creation of formal sector businesses, which are best suited to the provision of on-the-job training. Second, employers often will take on the full cost of on-the-job training. One workable arrangement can be for the cost of training to be bourn by both employer and employee: a lowered wage is paid during the period of on-the-job training. But in Nicaragua today, the structure of minimum wages is so high relative to actual paid wages that there is virtually no room for a negotiated temporary lower wage while a worker receives training. Policy makers should make it possible for employers to offer a negotiated, temporarily lowered wage, lower than the official minimum, for training purposes. Also, as mentioned above, policy makers may want to avoid indexing the minimum wage to the exchange rate, because such indexing will further discourage producers from offering formal employment.

■ The wedge between the price of labor paid by producers and the net wage earned by workers is unnecessarily high. Efforts to decrease the burden of the payroll tax must be given high priority. More generally, the current structure of incentives discourages the creation of formal sector businesses. The present set of tariffs and subsidies that gives different treatment to different sectors of the economy, and even to different commodities within sectors, has to be replaced by a uniform, low tariff (and ideally no subsidies) so as to minimize the distortions in relative prices that exist today. The current business environment encourages agricultural producers to seek special protections for their specific activity by rewarding lobbying activities. Ideally, their efforts would be spent trying to increase the productivity of their agricultural businesses instead.

4

RISK MANAGEMENT
INSTRUMENTS

Lacking Risk-Management Resources: The Vicious Cycle

A series of negative weather-related and price-related shocks have overlapped and exacerbated each other in Nicaragua in recent years—making it extremely difficult or impossible to isolate their impacts. These shocks include Hurricane Mitch, which caused widespread destruction in 1998, erratic rainfall and persistent drought over the past few years, and the decline in international commodity prices for major export crops (notably the steep decline in coffee prices) and competing import crops (which result in downward pressure on domestic prices), along with increases in the prices of imported petroleum products (for example, fuel and fertilizer). Furthermore, there has been a global economic downturn in recent years, especially since September 11, 2001. Thus, there are several negative forces simultaneously sweeping rural areas in Nicaragua, and neighboring Central American countries, and they are occurring at a time when many poor rural Nicaraguan households are extremely vulnerable to additional shocks, because their assets bases and risk management capacities have been reduced.[23]

Lacking appropriate risk management instruments due to poorly functioning or absent labor, finance (credit and savings) and insurance markets (along with uncertain land rights) creates short- and long-term actual and opportunity costs. Since households must "self-insure" they tend to use low-risk/low-return production practices that result in "losses" in potential income. [24] Estimates are that such production decisions might result in a 15–20 percent loss in income for smallholders, who are reluctant to adopt improved technologies (MAGFOR 1999). Furthermore, there is a cycle of poverty that results, because of low incomes and assets, when shocks do strike, these households

---

23. Indeed, all of the countries neighboring Nicaragua, including Costa Rica, El Salvador, Guatemala, and Honduras are experiencing similar crises (see IBD/WB/USAID, 2002; USAID, 2002). This also impacts Nicaragua, by limiting cross-border trade and labor migration opportunities.

24. For example, inter-cropping and multi-cropping, scattering of fields and staggering of planting dates, use of low yielding traditional varieties that might be more resistant to weather-related risks and pests/diseases.

are poorly positioned to manage the risks and often need to resort to actions that further degrade their own asset bases (selling assets, cutting down trees, taking children out of school, cutting back on health expenditures) and can impose costs on the rest of society. And this often occurs when government is least able to increase social expenditures.

Medium and larger farmers who are more commercially oriented in their production and marketing also must, in many cases, resort to "self-insurance" due to the lack of well-functioning rural financial services and the absence of agricultural insurance. However, they have a stronger asset base to draw upon in times of emergency, and they usually are located in more favorable agroecological zones and have better access to infrastructure and agricultural support services. Also, they are a more formidable political lobbying group, which helps get the attention of government in times of need, which in turn can help them get assistance. It is important to note that medium and larger farmers are major employers of agricultural labor (many whom are small grain farmers or coffee producers), thus the welfare of the former also impacts the welfare of the latter.

The human and physical costs of a shock can increase rapidly if not dealt with in a timely manner. Declining public revenues in the aftermath of shocks leave everyone worse off and can ignite a vicious cycle of rising poverty and a weaker nation, and possibly culminating in social unrest. Nicaragua has relied on the international donor community for assistance in financing the costs of relief and reconstruction and such dependence is likely to continue, to some degree. However, domestic counterpart resources are needed to gain emergency relief coordination and leadership especially when shocks occur, since it takes time for the international community to get mobilized, and for medium-term investments after the targeted donor assistance programs have ended. As such, as part of its efforts to make the agricultural sector an engine of growth, Government of Nicaragua recognizes it needs to find ways to incorporate sustainable self-protection into comprehensive disaster risk management strategy).

An Overview of Major Rainfall-Related Risks

There is considerable concern that rainfall patterns, influenced largely by the El Niño Southern Oscillation (ENSO), are changing in Nicaragua and that extreme rainfall events (droughts and floods) are increasing in terms of their frequency and severity, thereby increasing the risks associated with these events. In addition, because of environmental degradation and increasing land area devoted to agricultural production (through rehabilitation of agricultural land or clearing of land) and movement to higher value agricultural enterprises, the exposure to risks and the value at risk are both increasing.

Droughts and floods in Nicaragua tend to occur in specific geographic locations, notably in the Departments of Leon, Chinandega, the Segovias (and to a lesser extent parts of Esteli, Matagalpa and Jinotega).[25] However, it is difficult to generalize the geographic spread of droughts or floods because there can be large differences in rainfall over relatively small areas, and there are many other factors such as soil moisture and water holding capacity, vegetative cover, elevation and slope, and stage of crop development when rainfall deficits or excesses occur, etc. that determine whether too little or too much rainfall might actually result in drought or flood conditions for a given farm location.[26] In addition, total accumulated rainfall in a given season provides a deceptive image of water deficiency or excess for agricultural production (Rojas, Rodríguez, and Rivas 2000). This has led Nicaraguan farmers to adopt flexible farming practices (for example, in terms of field, crop, and variety selection) that are suited to soil moisture and rainfall patterns. For exam-

---

25. A majority of Nicaragua's rural population and agricultural activity takes in these Departments. According to Freeman et. al. (2000) the Pacific region, notably Leon and Chinandega, are mainly affected by water- and weather-related phenomena, and they are Nicaragua's poorest regions.

26. A recent study that tried to identify zones at greatest risk to deficit and excess rainfall found that they are located in a triangle enclosing the area between the meteorological stations located in Chinandega, Jinotega and Matagalpa (see Rojas, et. al., 2000).

ple, because of the bimodal rainfall distribution Nicaraguan farmers plan different planting seasons: Primera (May to August), Postrerón (June to October), Postrera (mid-August to November), and Apante (from November to February). Planting decisions for each period depend on accumulated soil moisture and rainfall during critical times during a given period.[27]

In terms of economic importance for the agricultural sector and household food security, Primera and Postrera periods are most important. Both periods are prone to droughts, but the primera season is more drought prone.[28] The Apante period is important for food security, notably the planting of maize and beans.

Variability in Production and Profitability

As mentioned previously, the Departments of León, Chinandega, and the Segovias are prone to rainfall variability, which can result in variability of planting areas and yields. Clearly there are other factors that influence farmers' production decisions and yields (for example, prices for outputs and inputs, available technology, and relative crop profitability).[29] However, it is interesting to note that a recent analysis of production area, yields and total production for all of Nicaragua, and the Departments of Leon, Chinandega, and Nueva Segovia found significant year-to-year variability in production area, yields and total production from 1990/1 to 1998/99 for maize, beans, rice, peanut, sesame, sorghum, and soybean (Siegel 2000). This high variability in area planted, yield and total production is important since Leon and Chinandega are major national producers of peanut, soybean and sesame (they account for over 90 percent of national production on average) and sorghum (they account for almost 40 percent of national production on average). Commercial framers use the high variability mechanism in response to variations in domestic demand (for example, soybeans) and international prices (for example, peanuts).

It is also important to analyze the relationship between farm-level profitability and potential rainfall-related yield reductions. An analysis of crop budgets for the year 2000[30], that considered three levels of technology for each crop found that, in most cases, net revenues were 20–40 percent of gross revenues[31], which indicates that even with a 20 percent shortfall in yields, farmers should be able to cover their costs of production (i.e., expenditures on purchased inputs).[32] Thus, farmers could, in theory, repay input loans. On the other hand, with a 20 percent shortfall in yield, farmers would receive lower returns to own-labor and land, which could result in cash flow problems and result in an inability to repay loans (and to invest in inputs for the following season). Alternatively (assuming there was no crop insurance), farmers would need to draw on alternative income sources or asset sales to repay loans and smooth consumption and be able to invest in inputs for the following

---

27. Rainfall tends to be more intense during the Postrera period, and the critical times are October and November. However, if rainfall was abundant in September, crops might not be so negatively impacted by deficit rainfall during October-November (see Rojas, et. al., 2000).

28. A recent analysis/modeling exercise identified about 12 occurrences of drought from 1970 to 1999, with 8 occurring during Primera and 4 during Postrera (see Rojas, et. al., 2000).

29. Although the vast majority of the farmers in these Departments are small farmers (many of them producing mainly focusing on basic grain production for home consumption), there are also larger commercial farmers. These larger commercial farmers are important producers of many crops and are also major employers of agricultural laborers (many of them in turn, are small farmers).

30. See Siegel (2000) for details and World Bank (2001) for summary of results and the implications for trying to implement rainfall insurance.

31. Net revenues were calculated as gross revenues minus outlays on purchased inputs (including hired labor), but excluding returns to own labor and management, and land. Costs of production vary greatly by crop and by technology (mechanized, mechanized-oxen, hand-oxen).

32. This assumes that the change in yield does not result in a change in output prices. Which, as commodity markets are increasingly liberalized might not be so unrealistic. However, as mentioned later in the discussion of commodity price risks, there is ample evidence of market segmentation, especially in remote rural areas that would result in changes in local commodity prices if there was a significant change in production (especially of basic grains that are consumed domestically, compared to export commodities).

BOX 4: A SHORT-TERM PHENOMENON OR A LONG-TERM CRISIS?

A recent USAID (2002) report updating the situation notes: Rainfall in 2001 was erratic and unevenly distributed throughout the drought area. Conditions through the first planting cycle (May-August, 2001) resulted in losses in the corn and bean crops in Nicaragua and led to transitory food insecurity. The second harvest (February-March 2002) was spotty, with wide variations in production. This aggravated an already difficult situation, since over 50 percent of the population are poor and chronically food insecure. Availability of seeds was a problem in some areas and may be again in the coming 2002 planting season, especially if El Niño returns, as indications strongly suggest. Approximately 20 percent of the second harvest crops were lost and a further 10-15 percent were seriously stressed, greatly lowering yields; the overall area cultivated was also decreased by 17 percent from recent averages. The effects are particularly evident in the traditionally drier areas of northern and central Nicaragua. USAID estimates that food reserves in many households will run out several months prior to the next crop harvest, and the shortage will be most pronounced in June, July, and August. Household incomes have also suffered from the coffee crisis and the lower demand for coffee laborers {note: many of small farmers from Leon, Chinandega and Esteli usually work in coffee harvests in Matagalpa). Moreover, many small-scale farmers in the drought prone areas lack resources to purchase basic agricultural inputs, such as improved seeds and fertilizers, for the coming season. In addition, there is an increased threat of forest fires because of the dry weather and bark beetle infestation. *The drought, however, is a short-term phenomenon linked to the longer-term crisis in the rural economy as a result of its negative effects on household food security.*

season. In most cases, net revenues are less than or equal to 40–50 percent of gross revenues, which indicates that with a 40–50 percent shortfall in yields, farmers would not be able to cover their costs of production and would experience serious difficulties in repaying loans, smoothing consumption, and investing in inputs for the following season - if they did not receive some compensation through insurance or assistance from other sources. Thus, based on these results it be important to analyze the costs and benefits of crop insurance for yield losses above 15–20 percent, and especially above 40–50 percent. The 20 percent yield loss threshold is important, because some recent studies trying to define a drought have used a 20 percent rainfall deficit as a threshold for drought (although a 20 percent rainfall deficit does not necessarily translate into a 20 percent yield loss).

Recurrent Droughts

Recurrent droughts affect large parts of Nicaragua, causing considerable crop losses and subsequent hardships for many rural households. Many smallholder producers of food staple grains have been directly impacted, and the demand for agricultural labor (by medium and large sized farms) also declined. The Departments of León, Chinandega, Estelí, and Matagalpa have been particularly affected. Many areas are also facing increased risks of forest fires (and there have been numerous forest fires reported) as a result of the drought.

Despite the very bleak situation that the USAID report presents, it concludes that the drought is really a "short-term phenomena" that is actually linked to the "longer-term crisis" in the rural economy. Clearly it is critical to deal with both the short-term and long-term risks and crises facing the rural sector. The next section reviews some of the risks and crises that are primarily being driven by commodity price risks.

Commodity Price-Related Risks

During the 1990s, like many other developing countries, the Government of Nicaragua took the decision to liberalize its economy to allow prices of commodities to float freely, both domestic- and export-oriented commodities as well as agricultural inputs.[33] As such, levels and fluctuations in

---

33. Notable exceptions are tariffs remaining on some basic grains such as maize, rice and sorghum.

domestic prices are more closely related to levels and fluctuations of international prices. The new market openness, which is supposed to promote improved allocation of resources and increased competitiveness, has left farmers (and consumers) more exposed to international commodity markets and prices than previously, when the Nicaraguan Government had a more active role in setting producer/consumer prices and had public sector commodity marketing boards to stabilize marketed quantities and prices.

During the 1990s there has been a general trend towards declining international commodity prices and fluctuations in these prices around the downward trend. For example, during the 1990s, the average variation in maize prices has been plus/minus 17 percent (ranging from high of +/- 39 percent to a low of +/-4 percent annual price variation), and the average variation in coffee prices plus/minus 26 percent (ranging from high of +/- 79 percent to a low of +/-10 percent annual price variation). From 1999 to 2002 the decline in domestic maize prices was about 15–20 percent and for coffee more than 50 percent.

Significant differences in commodity prices still exist within Nicaragua, due to domestic market imperfections that result in market segmentation. For example, commodity price levels and fluctuations in some remote rural areas are closer related to local production scarcities and surpluses because of the lack of transport infrastructure and storage capacity. It is important to note that one of the most successful programs initiated by the Nicaraguan Government in recent years has been the promotion of small-scale "backyard" grain storage ("silos metálicos") using very simple technology. The improved storage has helped small farmers obtain higher prices since they do not need to rush to make sales at harvest time when prices tend to be at their lowest point. It also allows farmers to manage price risks. In addition, it has cut storage losses, which allows farmers to better manage their food security.

For a good example of how commodity prices are fluctuating from year-to-year, along with volumes of production and value of exports, see the table below that compares 2000 to 2001. A notable change took place in coffee, where international prices declined by 50 percent and coffee exports declined by about 20 percent, largely due to cuts in production as a response to low prices. As a result, and the value of coffee exports fell by 43 percent. The decline in value of coffee exports by about US$95 million (as coffee's share of total exports fell from 26 percent to 13 percent). This decline is extremely significant considering that total exports were about US$645 and US$605 million in 2000 and 2001, respectively (US$95 million is 15 percent of US$615 million). Changes in both coffee prices and yields exacerbated the fluctuation in the value of coffee exports, and the US$95 million "loss" in export income have had important macroeconomic and microeconomic impacts.

Prices of sesame also experienced a dramatic decline from 2000 to 2001, declining by 46 percent. In contrast to coffee, sesame production and exports actually increased, so the overall negative impact on export value was 39 percent. For sesame producers the steep decline in prices had a large negative impact on farm income. However, in contrast to coffee, from a macroeconomic perspective the impacts were minimal since sesame exports account for less than 1 percent of total exports. International prices for tobacco also experienced a steep decline (-86 percent), and production/exports declined by about (21 percent), resulting in a decline in value of exports of 86 percent. Like sesame, the price fall had important impacts on tobacco producers (and tobacco laborers), but not much of a macroeconomic impact.

One "sweet change" that took place from 2000 to 2001 was the increase in sugar prices (+22) and the even larger increase in sugar production/exports (+61 percent). These combined effects resulted in an increase in value of sugar exports by 96 percent to a total export value of about US$56 million.[34] Thus, compared to the value of coffee exports, sugar was about 17 percent of the value of coffee exports in 2000 and 73 percent in 2001. Quite a change! Similarly, peanut exports

---

34. It should be noted that there are special international arrangements for sugar exports, like import quotas by the USA and EU. Thus, the price of sugar is not all determined through international commodity markets.

TABLE 19: COMMODITY PRICES, VOLUMES AND EXPORT VALUE FOR AGRICULTURE, LIVESTOCK AND EXPORTS									
	2000			**2001**			**% Change**		
Export Item	**Price in US$/mt**	**Volume '000 mt**	**Value US$ mil**	**Price US$/mt**	**Volume '000 mt**	**Value US$ mil**	**Price/mt**	**Volume**	**Value**
1. Agriculture			267,454			181,551			-32
			(41%)			(30%)			
Coffee	95.9	1,758	169,580	55.0	1,392	76,556	-43	-21	-55
Sesame	44.3	85	3,778	24.1	95	2,300	-46	+12	-39
Sugar	8.3	3,463	28,745	10.1	5,573	56,308	+22	+61	+96
Banana	4.9	1,771	8,678	5.0	2,197	10,987	+2	+24	+27
Tobacco	1,229.3	26	32,453	236.9	21	4,900	-81	-19	-85
Peanut	30.2	801	24,219	30.6	996	30,500	+1	+24	+26
2. Livestock			94,700			104,300			+10
			(15%)			(17%)			
Meat	1.0	50,300	52,400	1.1	59,200	65,600	+10	+30	+25
Live Animals	281.6	72	20,300	307.5	75	23,000	+9	+13	+13
Dairy Prod.			22,000			15,700			-29
3. Traditional Agr and Livestock (1 + 2)			362,154 (56%)			285,851 (47%)			-21
4. Other Agr and Livestock			47,220 (7%)			55,710 (9%)			+18
5. All Other Exports			235,742 (37%)			264,081 (44%)			+12
TOTAL EXPORTS			645,116 (100%)			605,642 (100%)			-6

Source: MAGFOR 2002.

increased from 2000 to 2001, as prices remained fairly stable (+1 percent), but exports increased by 24 percent from about US$24 to US$30 million.

When comparing livestock to crop exports and non-agricultural to agricultural exports, it can be observed that from 2000 to 2001: a) livestock prices, export volumes, and export values increased by about 10 percent, and b) non-agricultural exports increased by 12 percent. As such, the share of livestock products in total exports increased from 15 percent to 17 percent and the share of non-agricultural exports increased by 12 percent. This is in contrast to the decline in agricultural exports by 32 percent and a decline in share from 41 percent to 30 percent.[35]

As the example presented in this section demonstrates, the significant changes in coffee prices, export volumes, and export value have potentially significant macroeconomic and microeconomic impacts on Nicaragua.

---

35. It should be noted that this change in shares might be viewed as some as an example of how Nicaragua's export portfolio is "diversifying" and a positive development. However, such de facto diversification is really a shrinkage of the economic base and not a reallocation of resources to achieve higher returns to existing assets and factors of production.

Suggested Areas for Action

In the short term, there is a need for emergency relief efforts to help the poorest and most vulnerable individuals and households suffering from ongoing shocks and crises in the agricultural sector. Improved targeting and self-targeting strategies are needed for farmers, laborers and others directly and indirectly impacted by the ongoing crises. It would be best if some of these short-term safety net efforts could be directed towards risk reduction activities to provide some longer term benefits to households. The Nicaraguan Government should work closely with donors and NGOs to make sure that emergency relief efforts provide positive short and longer-term incentives for improving risk management and decreasing vulnerability. The Emergency Social Funds (FISE) Project and community-based social funds could be one option for use.

In the longer term, there are several areas for action to be suggested. Perhaps among the most promising are schemes for providing agricultural insurance through rural finance institutions.

Providing Agricultural Insurance Through Rural Finance Institutions

The World Bank is carrying out pilot studies in Nicaragua on both rainfall insurance (see World Bank 2001a; 2002c) and commodity price insurance for coffee (Varangis, Larson, Anderson 2002), with a view towards implementing pilot projects. These insurance schemes constitute a potential "win-win" opportunity for agricultural banks and therefore should be seriously pursued by policy makers and the managers of agricultural and rural banks.

Well-designed agricultural insurance schemes have two basic advantages: a) they enable farmers to feel more comfortable to specialize in production, which is extremely important to facilitate the adoption of more advanced high risk- high return technologies, and b) by reducing variance in producers' incomes, they reduce risks for their creditors, enabling lenders to provide more credit at lower interest rates. Indeed, well-designed insurance products can substitute for more traditional forms of collateral and thereby allow creditors to lend to small-scale farmers who would otherwise be considered bad risks and therefore have no access to formal credit.

The main challenge is how to overcome the complex issues of moral hazard and adverse selection that have been the stumbling block of both private and public initiatives in agricultural insurance, not to mention the governance issues that have bankrupted most public crop insurance schemes. Worldwide, there are few successful public programs that provide farm-level insurance. However, fruitful theoretical developments are beginning to be piloted with two financial instruments. The first is modern commodity price risk management mechanisms- a joint product of a loan with a put option on the price of the commodity concerned, and the second is weather-based index insurance. Taken together, these can constitute an important component of a comprehensive rural finance strategy that, in addition to its direct benefits, could facilitate expansion of unsubsidized agricultural credit to clients that were considered until now not credit worthy by for profit lenders.

Past strategies to manage *commodity price risk* such as international commodity agreements (for coffee), marketing boards, and price controls have proven to be largely ineffective. Indeed, in a vast number of cases they have simply proven to be a substantial tax on producers and have therefore depressed production. Many developing countries have therefore moved toward a policy framework of liberalized trading environments to enhance producer incentives and improve the efficiency of the commodity marketing sector. In this context, modern options mechanisms available in international commodity markets have proven to be an alternative approach by which rural producers can manage risks. In particular, put options allow producers to set a market-determined floor price (in effect, a guaranteed minimum price) they can expect to receive at the end of a crop season, while reaping the benefits of upside price movements.[36]

---

36. A prerequisite to implement these market based price hedging instruments is state elimination of the support price for the commodity concerned and that there be a liquid commodity exchange where the risk can be laid off.

Weather-Based Index Insurance provides an incentive-compatible alternative to standard crop insurance schemes to help farmers mitigate production risks. In essence they constitute contracts involving payment of an actuarially calculated premium that result in a payout under the scheme in the event of specific clear outcomes (for example, rainfall below a given critical quantity during a specific predetermined period—say 30 days of the critical cropping season, or when yields over a given area fall substantially below long term average values). In years when the insured event occurs, all the insured people who purchased the insurance receive the same payment per unit of insurance, *irrespective* of the actual damage to their crops and income that resulted from the low rainfall or their individual yield. This instrument is designed to overcome the issues of moral hazard and adverse selection that presently plague the traditional insurance programs. Rainfall and area yield can be verified by independent systems that do not require the monitoring of each claimant (individual farms) for individual damages and indemnification.

This scheme has the advantage that (i) it avoids all moral hazard and adverse selection problems; (ii) it is relatively inexpensive to administer, as there are no individual contracts to write and no on-farm inspections are needed; (iii) the insurance can be sold to anyone and not only to farmers (it can and should preferably be sold to all those whose income is correlated with the insured event); (iv) it can easily be run by the private sector; (v) when not subsidized, as it should be, it will only be purchased if it is considered less expensive or more effective than alternative risk management strategies; (vi) a secondary market for insurance certificates could emerge, which would encourage adjustments as the crop season develops; and (vii) it could relieve the government from the need to assist farmers in the event of severe droughts or a substantial decline in yields.

Revenue insurance, a combination of price and yield insurance, is really what interests farmers, farmers' association (cooperatives) and financial intermediaries. Because it is revenues—or more correctly net income—that is of interest. The simplest way to provide revenue insurance is by bundling price and weather insurance. More sophisticated revenue insurance can be designed.

To package the insurance product, a well-established rural financial intermediary (RFI) could aggregate the demand for commodity price and/or weather insurance of small farmers in order to meet the contract transaction standards in the liquid commodity exchanges of developed countries. This RFI can hopefully perform this task utilizing sunk costs already incurred to establish relationships with borrowers. For such a RFIs, adding price risk insurance to a standard loan agreement requires low transaction costs. While transaction costs would be low, the benefits could be significant for the RFI: (i) it would diversify its products, thereby, providing better service to its target clientele, (ii) improve the financial discipline by increasing loan recovery and reducing non performing loans, (iii) create a market for risk that could be reflected in differential lending rates distinguishing between clients with price risk insurance and those lacking it, and (iv) improve access to credit and its terms including transforming clients from "non creditworthy" status to "credit worthy" because they have acquired price risk insurance.

Since the value of commodities produced by individual small farmers is significantly lower than the value of standard contracts traded in international (or domestic) commodity exchanges, it would be prohibitive to sell put options as separate, small-denomination products to small-scale producers. However, by coupling a put option as a joint product with credit and other financial products, transaction costs can be reduced significantly for the creditor and the rural producer alike.

Moreover, creditors are able to take advantage of the synergy that is created between insurance components and credit enhancement as it not only provides an additional source of fee-based revenue but also improves the quality of the loan portfolio by eliminating or substantially reducing unwilling defaults, which in turn benefits borrowing producers through improved access to finance. Further benefits arise when there is a secondary market for the options instruments, allowing for re-pricing of risks during the cropping season, and for the participation of a broader range of investors in financing rural production. This is the direction in which many RFIs could improve their financial performance, expand their variety of financial products offered to their clientele, increase their outreach to clientele not served before as a result of inability to manage the associated credit risk.

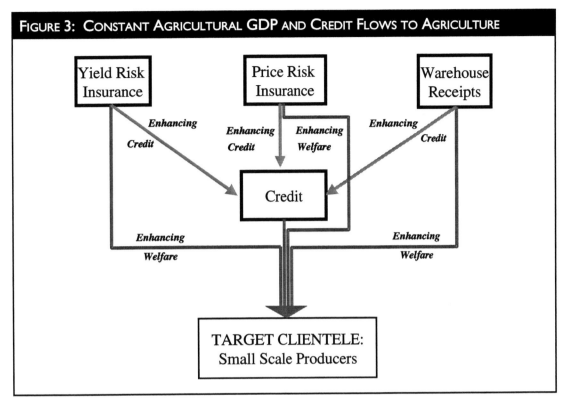

FIGURE 3: CONSTANT AGRICULTURAL GDP AND CREDIT FLOWS TO AGRICULTURE

Source: Yaron, RDVCG, 2001.

Other Steps To Take

Besides the linking of insurance to rural finance, there are several other areas for action to consider:

Improving rural financial institutions (RFIs—such as commercial banks, microfinance institutions, cooperatives) and encouraging/helping them to offer innovative insurance product, alongside credit services. There is also a need to focus attention on the risk management needs of the RFIs themselves. Ongoing pilot studies on the provision of both weather-based insurance and commodity-price insurance through rural finance institutions are discussed at the end of Chapter III. Insurance could be better integrated into a new, comprehensive rural finance strategy.

Improving forecasting, early warning and monitoring systems for agricultural risks, risk management practices, and outcomes. Improved information on weather patterns, soil moisture, agroecological conditions etc. are needed to better forecast events that might negatively impact households. More information is needed on households' risk management strategies and capacities. Such information should help in efforts to reduce risks and reduce the impacts of such events. The Agricultural Technology Project can be mobilized for this purpose. Also, initiatives should be coordinated with other ministries (for example, MARENA, IDA) and organizations (for example, INITER).

Improving knowledge about risks and risk management strategies for given groups of households, communities and localities. Better knowledge gathering allows better targeted investments to facilitate local risk reduction efforts and to organize a priori emergency relief and rehabilitation programs. The Natural Disaster Vulnerability Project and Rural Municipalities Project are good examples of such knowledge gathering.

Coordinating agricultural production technologies, post-harvest activities and land-use patterns with activities related to environmental conservation, protection and enhancement. Agricultural and environmental risks and risk management have a great deal in common, and these commonalities should be formalized so that sustainable economic and environmental practices are promoted. The Forestry Project and Agricultural Technology Project should identify overlaps and gaps.

Recognizing the critical potential role of agricultural technology in managing agricultural risks and to mainstream and operationalize agricultural risk management into the Agricultural Technology Project. This possibility was already reviewed in a recent Supervision Report for the project. It will require a more holistic farming systems approach and conscious efforts to utilize appropriate technologies to achieve both economic and environmental sustainability. Drought resistant technologies and improved water management practices for cash crops and food staples, along with improved storage and post-harvest technologies are examples. It is also critical to have a coordinated plan to improve education, research and training with respect to risk management options.

Further improving the design and delivery of safety net systems, including improved targeting and monitoring systems. Other considerations include the use of agricultural insurance such as weather based insurance and commodity price insurance as a means to fund safety net programs and to deliver assistance to the most vulnerable agricultural households.

Considering the importance of risk and risk management when considering other areas dealt with in this paper, such as: stability in macroeconomic and policy regime, secure land tenure and use, flexible labor markets and labor mobility, improved marketing, transport and communications infrastructure.

REFERENCES

Aráuz, Alejandro. 2001. "Carga Impositiva del Sector Agropecuario." Paper prepared for Programa de Fortalecimiento de las Capacidades del Sector Privado para la Formulación de Políticas. (PROVIA-IICA-USAID), Managua, Nicaragua. Processed.

———. 2002. "Análisis preliminar del Marco de Incentivos del Sector Agropecuario." World Bank. Background Paper for the Agriculture and Economic Sector Work. Managua, Nicaragua.

Arcia, Gustavo. 2000. "Education and Poverty in Nicaragua." Background Paper for the Nicaragua Poverty Assessment. World Bank. Report 20488, Washington, D.C.

Austin, James E. 2000. "Leader to Leader." Drucker Foundation and Jossey-Bass Inc., San Francisco.

Berdegue, John, Thomas Reardon and S. Escobar. 2001. *World Development*, Vol. 29, No.3.

Budinich, Ema. 2001. "Revisión del Gasto Público del Sector Rural." World Bank. Background Paper for the Public Expenditure Review.

BCN (Banco Central de Nicaragua). 2001. "Valor Agregado Calendario." Managua, Nicaragua.

———. 2002. "Indicadores Económicos." Managua, Nicaragua.

CEI (Centro de Promoción de Exportaciones e Inversión Extranjera). 2002. "Investors Guide: Nicaragua 2000–2001". Managua, Nicaragua.

Chiquita 2000 Bands International, Corporate Social Responsibility Report.

Corral, Leonardo, and Thomas Reardon. 2001. "Rural Non-farm and Farm Incomes in Nicaragua: Evidence." *World Development*. Vol.29, No.3.

Davis, Benjamin, and Rinku Murgai. 2000. "Between Poverty and Prosperity: Rural Households in Nicaragua." Background Paper for the Nicaragua Poverty Assessment. World Bank. Report 20488, Washington, D.C.

Flores M., and others. 2002. "Centroamérica: El Impacto de la Caída de los Precios del Café." ECLAC. *Estudios y Perspectivas*. Mexico.

Food and Agriculture Organization (FAO). 2001. "Analysis of the Medium-term Effects of Hurricane Mitch on Food Security in Central America." Rome, Italy.

Foster, William, and Alberto Valdés. 2002. "On the Domestic Management of Price Risk in the Context of Trade Reform in LDCs." Prepared for the International Agricultural Trade Research Consortium and the World Bank, the Developing Countries, and the WTO. June 16th-17th. Vancouver. Canada.

Foster, William, and Alberto Valdés. 2001. "Have Reforms Failed in Agriculture? The Case of Latin America." World Bank. Washington, D.C.

Freeman, Paul, and others. 2000. "Integrating Natural Catastrophe Exposure into Development Planning: Case Study of Natural Catastrophe Risk in Nicaragua." International Institute for Applied Systems Analysis (IIASA). Laxenburg, Austria.

Grayson, David 2002, and Adrian Hodges. "Everybody's Business." DK Publishing Inc., New York.

Galindo, Arturo, and Margaret Miller. 2001."Can Credit Registries Reduce Credit Constraints?" Inter-American Development Bank Research Department. Prepared for the Annual Meetings of the Board of Governors. Santiago, Chile. Processed.

Gillespie, Nancy, and others. 2001. "Toward a Social Protection Strategy for Nicaragua: A Review of Selected Social Programs in the PRSP Portfolio." World Bank. Washington, D.C.

Ilahi, Nadim. 2002. "Labor Markets and Poverty Reduction". Background Paper for the Nicaragua Poverty Assessment. World Bank. Report 20488, Washington, D.C.

IDB (Inter-American Development Bank). 2001. "Transición Competitiva para el Café Centro-americano: Crisis Internacional del Café y su Impacto en Nicaragua." Informe Preliminar, Managua, Nicaragua.

IDB/WB/USAID. (Inter American Development Bank, The World Bank and The United States Development Agency). 2002. "Managing the Competitive Transition of the Coffee Sector in Central America." Discussion Document prepared for the Regional Workshop: The Coffee Crisis and its Impact in Central America: Situation and Lines of Action. April 3d-5th. Antigua, Guatemala.

INCAE (Instituto Centroamericano de Administración de Empresas). 2002. "Barreras a la Com-petitividad y Respuesta de Pequeños Productores Rurales." Managua, Nicaragua.

Jenkins and Shukla. 1997. "*Public Finance in Open Economies.*" Harvard University, Harvard International Tax Program, June 1997.

Kruger, Diana. 2000. "Distributional Effects of Agricultural Incentives Policies in Nicaragua." Background Paper for the Nicaragua Poverty Assessment. World Bank. Report 20488, Washington, D.C.

———. 2000. "Rates of Return to Education". Background Paper for the Nicaragua Poverty Assessment. World Bank. Report 20488, Washington, D.C.

Lachler, Ulrich. 2001. "A Growth Accounting Approach." Background Note for the Nicaragua Poverty Assessment. World Bank. Report 20488, Washington, D.C.

Legovini, Adriana. 2002 "The Distributional Impact Of Loans In Nicaragua." Managua, Nicaragua. Processed.

Leisinger, Klaus M. 2000, and Karin M.Schmitt. "Public-Private Partnership: Building a Com-mon Understanding." Global Forum on Agricultural Research, Document # GFAR/00/14, Dresden.

Lewis, Christopher, and Luis Sanchez. 2000. "Nicaragua Rainfall Insurance". Draft. World Bank. Report prepared by NetRisk for the Rainfall Insurance Project.

Linder, Stephen H. 2000, and Pauline Vaillancourt Rosenau. "Public-Private Policy Partnerships." MIT Press, Boston.

MAGFOR (Ministry of Agriculture). 1999. "Of Potholes, Mudslides and Crossroads: Reflections and Implications of Natural Disasters for the Development of Rural Nicaragua." Managua. Nicaragua.

———. 2001a. "Bases para un Plan de Desarrollo Rural de Nicaragua: Una Propuesta para la Discusión y para la Acción." Universidad Centroamericana. Managua, Nicaragua.

———. 2001b. "Políticas para el Sector Agropecuario Forestal Nicaragüense, Ciclo Agrícola 2001/02." Managua, Nicaragua.

———. 2002a. "Del Manejo de la Crisis al Manejo del Riesgo en el Sector Agropecuario y Forestal." Presentation. Managua, Nicaragua.

———. 2002b. "Servicio de Información de Precios y Mercado". Managua, Nicaragua.

Morduch, Jonathan. 2001. "Rainfall Insurance and Vulnerability: Economic Principles and Cautionary Notes." World Bank. Background Note for the Rainfall Insurance Project for Nicaragua. Processed.

Nusselder, Hans, and Arie Sanders. 2002. "La Maduración de las Microfinanzas en Nicaragua: Oportunidades y Desafíos." Versión I. Centro de Estudios para el Desarrollo Rural/Free University of Amersterdam. San José, Costa Rica.

PPP 1999. "Public Private Partnership: A Guide for Local Government." Ministry of Municipal Affairs, British Columbia

PROVIA (Programa de Fortalecimiento de las Capacidades del Sector Privado para la Formulación de Políticas). 2001. "Estrategia para el Desarrollo Agropecuario y Forestal." Managua, Nicaragua.

———. 2001. "Los Incentivos de Producción: las Políticas de Comercio." Draft, Managua, Nicaragua.

———. 2002. "The Challenges Faced by the Agricultural Sector." Background Paper for the Agriculture and Economic Sector Work. Managua, Nicaragua.

Reyes J. 2002, and N. Twose. "Education-focused Corporate Social Responsibility in El Salvador." World Bank Technical Assistance Study. Washington DC.

Robinson, Margerite. 2001. "*The Microfinance Revolution: Sustainable Finance for the Poor.*" World Bank. Open Society Institute. New York.

Rodríguez, Juan F., and Diana Saavedra. 2000. "La deuda del Sector Agropecuario con el Sistema Bancario." Inter-American Development Bank. Managua, Nicaragua.

Rojas, Oscar, Jorge Rodriguez, and Roberto Rivas. 2000. "Agroclimatic Vulnerability and Rainfall Indices for the Insurance of Crops in Nicaragua." World Bank. Technical Feasibility Study for the Rainfall Insurance Project. Managua, Nicaragua.

Rose, Horacio J., and Oscar Neira. 1999. "Desempeño del Sector Agropecuario y Política de Incentivos. Elementos para una Política de Incentivos Sectorial." Analytical Paper for the Ministry of Agriculture. Managua, Nicaragua. Processed.

Ruben, Ruud, and D. van Strien. 2001. "Social Capital and Household Incomes in Nicaragua: The Economic Role of Rural Associations and Farmers' networks." Paper presented at the 74th EAAE.

Sánchez, Susana. 2001. "Financial Markets." Background Paper for the Nicaragua Poverty Assessment. World Bank. Report 20488.Washington, D.C.

SETEC (Secretaría Técnica de la Presidencia). 2000a. "A Strengthened Poverty Reduction Strategy." Managua, Nicaragua.

———. 2000b. "Poverty Map". Managua, Nicaragua.

Serpagli, Andrea. 2002. "A Review of the Main Constraints in the Oilseed, Coffee and Fruit and Vegetables Chains and an Action Plan to Overcome Them." World Bank. Background Paper for the Agriculture and Economic Sector Work. Washington, D.C.

Schiff, Maurice, and Alberto Valdés. 1992. The Political Economy of Agricultural Pricing Policy in Developing Countries, in Volume IV: A Synthesis of the Economics in Developing Countries, John Hopkins University Press, Baltimore, Maryland.

———. 1998. Policy Research Working Paper, No. 1967. World Bank, Washington, D.C.

Siegel, Paul. 2001. "Nicaragua Crops and Crop Budgets for Chinandega, León and Nueva Segovia." Draft. World Bank. Technical Assessment for the Rainfall Insurance Project. Washington, D.C. Processed.

SETEC 2002 "Rediseño de la Cartera de Programas de Apoyo Productivo en el área Rural de Nicaragua."

Sobrado, Carlos. 2000a. "Comparing Poverty for the Young and the Old." Background Note for the Nicaragua Poverty Assessment. World Bank. Report 20488, Washington, D.C.

———. 2000b. "The Determinants of Poverty in Nicaragua." Background Note for the Nicaragua Poverty Assessment. World Bank. Report 20488, Washington, D.C.

Starbucks 2001, Corporate Social Responsibility Annual Report.

Tollini, Helio. 1999. "Política de Innovación Tecnológica para Nicaragua." Technical Paper for the Ministry of Agriculture. Managua, Nicaragua. Processed.

USAID (United States Agency for International Development). 2002. "Central America in Crisis: USAID Response and Strategic Approach." Washington, D.C.

Ureta, Manuelita. 2002. "Rural Labor Markets in Nicaragua." Background Paper for the Agriculture and Economic Sector Work. World Bank. Washington, D.C.

Valdés, Alberto. 1998. "Trade Policy Reforms." World Bank Regional and Sector Studies, Washington, D.C.

———. 2001. "Nicaragua. A Note on the Incentives Framework for Agriculture. Material for a Policy Note." Santiago, Chile. Processed.

———. 2002. "Trade Liberalization versus Food Security? Observations on Latin America." *Quarterly Journal of International Agriculture*, Vol. 39, No. 4.

Valdés, Alberto, and William Foster. 2002. "Reflections On the Policy Implications of Agricultural Price Distortions and Price Transmission for Producers in Developing and Transition Economies." Prepared for the OECD/World Bank meeting on Agricultural Trade Reform, Adjustment and Poverty, Paris, May 23–24.

Valdés, Alberto, and Guillermo Bastos. 1999. "Reflexiones sobre el Sector Agrícola de Nicaragua con Enfasis en la Estructura de Incentivos." World Bank. Background Note for the Agriculture and Economic Sector Work.

Varangis, Panos, Donald Larson, and Jack Anderson. 2002. "Agricultural Markets and Risks: Management of the Latter, Not the Former." World Bank. Policy Research Working Paper #2793.

Vickers, Rob D., and Frank Baumgardt. 2002. "The State of Microfinance in Nicaragua." World Bank. Processed.

Wilhite, Donald. 2000. "Drought Mitigation in Nicaragua." World Bank. Technical Note for the Rainfall Insurance Project. National Drought Mitigation Center. Lincoln, Nebraska. Processed.

World Bank. 2000. "Ex-Post Evaluation of the Emergency Social Investment Fund." Washington, D.C.

———. 2000b. Agricultural Technology and Rural Training Project, Project Appraisal Document. Report No. 20168-NI. Washington, D.C.

World Bank. 2001a. "Nicaragua: Public Expenditure Review: Improving the Poverty Focus of Public Spending." Washington, D.C.

———. 2001b. "Natural Disaster Vulnerability Reduction: Project Appraisal Document." Report 21859-NI. Washington, D.C.

———. 2001c. "Nicaragua Poverty Assessment, Challenges and Opportunities for Poverty Reduction." Volume I: Main Volume. Report No. 20488-NI.

———. 2001d. "Regional Action Plan For Rural Development." Latin America and the Caribbean Region. An Input into the Revision of Vision to Action. Washington, D.C. Processed.

———. 2001e. "Feasibility Analysis for Developing Weather-based Index Insurance for Farmers and Intermediary Institutions in the Republic of Nicaragua." Report prepared by DECRG and FSD. Washington, D.C. Processed.

———. 2001f. "Nicaragua Agricultural Technology and Land Management Implementation Completion Report." Report No. 22547. Washington, D.C.

———. 2002 "Poverty Update." Managua, Nicaragua. Processed.

———. 2002a. "World Development Indicators." Washington, D.C.

———. 2002b. "Central American Region Dealing with the Coffee Crisis: Impacts and Strategies," Latin America and the Caribbean Regional Office (LCC2C). Washington, D.C. Processed.

———. 2002c. "Coffee Price Risk Management." Phase 2 Report. Washington, D.C.

———. 2002d. "Commodity Price Risk Management: Reducing Farmer Vulnerability." International Task Force on Commodity Price Risk Management. World Bank. Washington, D.C. Processed.

World Bank Institute 2001. "The e-course on Corporate Social Responsibility and Sustainable Competitiveness." Washington DC

Yaron, Jacob. 2001. "A note prepared for Presentation to the President of the World Bank on Commodity Price Risk Mitigation." The World Bank. Washington, D.C. Processed.